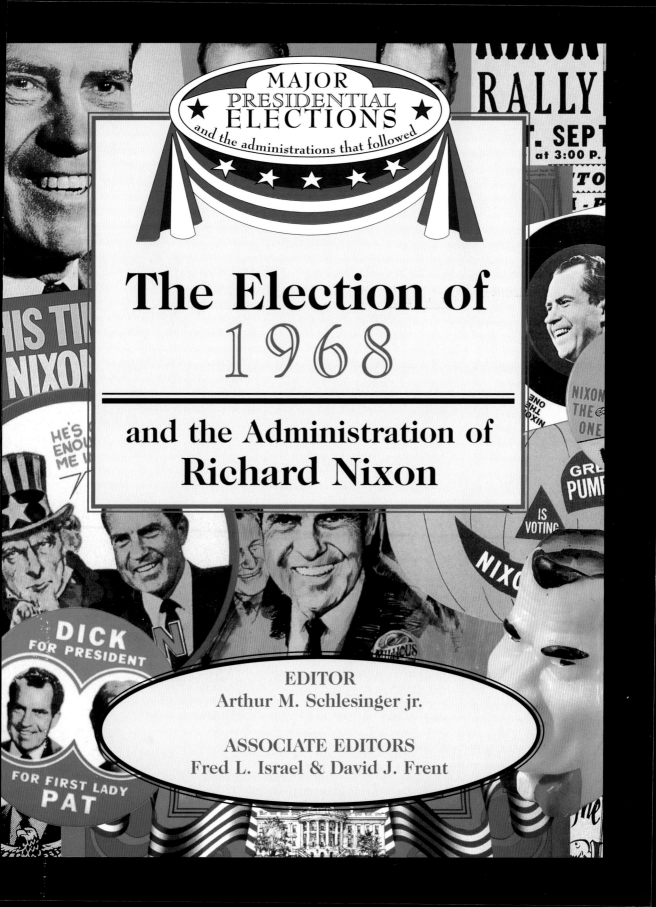

MAJOR PRESIDENTIAL ELECTIONS
★ and the administrations that followed ★

The Election of
1968

and the Administration of
Richard Nixon

EDITOR
Arthur M. Schlesinger jr.

ASSOCIATE EDITORS
Fred L. Israel & David J. Frent

The Elections of 1789 & 1792 and the Administration of George Washington

The Election of 1800 and the Administration of Thomas Jefferson

The Election of 1828 and the Administration of Andrew Jackson

The Election of 1840 and the Harrison/Tyler Administrations

The Election of 1860 and the Administration of Abraham Lincoln

The Election of 1876 and the Administration of Rutherford B. Hayes

The Election of 1896 and the Administration of William McKinley

The Election of 1912 and the Administration of Woodrow Wilson

The Election of 1932 and the Administration of Franklin D. Roosevelt

The Election of 1948 and the Administration of Harry S. Truman

The Election of 1960 and the Administration of John F. Kennedy

The Election of 1968 and the Administration of Richard Nixon

The Election of 1976 and the Administration of Jimmy Carter

The Election of 1980 and the Administration of Ronald Reagan

The Election of 2000 and the Administration of George W. Bush

The Election of
1968

and the Administration of Richard Nixon

EDITOR

Arthur M. Schlesinger, jr.
Albert Schweitzer Chair in the Humanities
The City University of New York

ASSOCIATE EDITORS

Fred L. Israel
Department of History
The City College of New York

David J. Frent
The David J. and Janice L. Frent
Political Americana Collection

Mason Crest Publishers
Philadelphia

Produced by OTTN Publishing, Stockton, New Jersey

Mason Crest Publishers
370 Reed Road
Broomall PA 19008
www.masoncrest.com

Research Consultant: Patrick R. Hilferty
Editorial Assistant: Jane Ziff

First printing

1 3 5 7 9 8 6 4 2

Library of Congress Cataloging-in-Publication Data

The election of 1968 and the administration of Richard Nixon / editor, Arthur M. Schlesinger, Jr. ;
associate editors, Fred L. Israel & David J. Frent.
    p. cm. — (Major presidential elections and the administrations that followed)
Summary: A discussion of the presidential election of 1968 and the subsequent administration of
Richard Nixon, based on source documents.
    Includes bibliographical references (p.) and index.
    ISBN 1-59084-362-2
1. Presidents—United States—Election—1968—Juvenile literature. 2. Presidents—United
States—Election—1968—Sources—Juvenile literature. 3. Nixon, Richard M. (Richard Milhous),
1913-   —Juvenile literature. 4. United States—Politics and government—1969-1974—Juvenile
literature. 5. United States—Politics and government—1969-1974—Sources—Juvenile literature.
[1. Presidents—Election—1968—Sources. 2. Nixon, Richard M. (Richard Milhous), 1913-   .
3. Elections. 4. United States—Politics and government—1969-1974—Sources.]   I. Schlesinger,
Arthur Meier, 1917-   . II. Israel, Fred L. III. Frent, David J. IV. Series.
E851.E44 2002
324.973'0923—dc21

                                                                                         2002012636

**Publisher's note: all quotations in this book come
from original sources, and contain the spelling and
grammatical inconsistencies of the original text.**

Table of Contents

★ INTRODUCTION ★
Arthur M. Schlesinger, Jr.

America suffers from a sort of intermittent fever—what one may call a quintan ague. Every fourth year there come terrible shakings, passing into the hot fit of the presidential election; then follows what physicians call "the interval"; then again the fit.

—James Bryce, *The American Commonwealth* (1888)

Running for president is the central rite in the American political order. It was not always so. *Choosing* the chief magistrate had been the point of the quadrennial election from the beginning, but it took a long while for candidates to *run* for the highest office in the land; that is, to solicit, visibly and actively, the support of the voters. These volumes show through text and illustration how those aspiring to the White House have moved on from ascetic self-restraint to shameless self-merchandising. This work thereby illuminates the changing ways the American people have conceived the role of their President. I hope it will also recall to new generations some of the more picturesque and endearing dimensions of American politics.

The primary force behind the revolution in campaign attitudes and techniques was a development unforeseen by the men who framed the Constitution—the rise of the party system. Party competition was not at all their original intent. Quite the contrary: inspired at one or two removes by Lord Bolingbroke's British tract of half a century earlier, *The Idea of a Patriot King*, the Founding Fathers envisaged a Patriot President, standing above party and faction, representing the whole people, offering the nation non-partisan leadership virtuously dedicated to the common good.

The ideal of the Patriot President was endangered, the Founding Fathers believed, by twin menaces—factionalism and factionalism's ugly offspring, the demagogue. Party competition would only encourage unscrupulous men to appeal to popular passion and prejudice. Alexander Hamilton in the 71st Federalist bemoaned the plight of the people, "beset as they continually are . . . by the snares of the ambitious, the avaricious, the desperate, by the artifices of men who possess their confidence more than they deserve it, and of those who seek to possess rather than to deserve it."

Pervading the Federalist was a theme sounded explicitly both in the first paper and the last: the fear that unleashing popular passions would bring on "the military despotism of a victorious demagogue." If the "mischiefs of faction" were, James Madison admitted in the Tenth Federalist, "sown in the nature of man," the object of politics was to repress this insidious disposition, not to yield to it. "If I could not go to heaven but with a party," said Thomas Jefferson, "I would not go there at all."

So the Father of his Country in his Farewell Address solemnly warned his countrymen against "the baneful effects of the spirit of party." That spirit, Washington conceded, was "inseparable from our nature"; but for popular government it was "truly their worst enemy." The "alternate domination of one faction over another," Washington said, would lead in the end to "formal and permanent despotism." The spirit of a party, "a fire not to be quenched . . . demands a uniform vigilance to prevent its bursting into a flame, lest, instead of warming, it should consume."

Yet even as Washington called on Americans to "discourage and restrain" the spirit of party, parties were beginning to crystallize around him. The eruption of partisanship in defiance of such august counsel argued that party competition might well serve functional necessities in the democratic republic.

After all, honest disagreement over policy and principle called for candid debate. And parties, it appeared, had vital roles to play in the consummation of the Constitution. The distribution of powers among three equal branches inclined the national government toward a chronic condition of stalemate. Parties offered the means of overcoming the constitutional separation of powers by coordinating the executive and legislative branches and furnishing the connective tissue essential to effective government. As national associations, moreover, parties were a force against provincialism and separatism. As instruments of compromise, they encouraged, within the parties as well as between them, the containment and mediation of national quarrels, at least until slavery broke the parties up. Henry D. Thoreau cared little enough for politics, but he saw the point: "Politics is, as it were, the gizzard of society, full of grit and gravel, and the two political parties are its two opposite halves, which grind on each other."

Furthermore, as the illustrations in these volumes so gloriously remind us, party competition was a great source of entertainment and fun—all the more important in those faraway days before the advent of baseball and football, of movies and radio and television. "To take a hand in the regulation of society and to discuss it," Alexis de Tocqueville observed when he visited America in the 1830s, "is his biggest concern and, so to speak, the only pleasure an American knows. . . . Even the women frequently attend public meetings and listen to political harangues as a recreation from their household labors. Debating clubs are, to a certain extent, a substitute for theatrical entertainments."

Condemned by the Founding Fathers, unknown to the Constitution, parties nonetheless imperiously forced themselves into political life. But the party system rose from the bottom up. For half a century, the first half-dozen Presidents continued to hold themselves above party. The disappearance of the Federalist Party after the War of 1812 suspended party competition. James Monroe, with no opponent at all in the election of 1820, presided proudly over the Era of Good Feelings, so called because there were no parties around to excite ill feelings. Monroe's successor, John Quincy Adams, despised electioneering and inveighed against the "fashion of peddling for popularity by traveling around the country gathering crowds together, hawking for public dinners, and spouting empty speeches." Men of the old republic believed presidential candidates should be men who already deserved the people's confidence rather than those seeking to win it. Character and virtue, not charisma and ambition, should be the grounds for choosing a President.

Adams was the last of the old school. Andrew Jackson, by beating him in the 1828 election, legitimized party politics and opened a new political era. The rationale of the new school was provided by Jackson's counselor and successor, Martin Van Buren, the classic philosopher of the role of party in the American democracy. By the time Van Buren took his own oath of office in 1837, parties were entrenched as the instruments of American self-government. In Van Buren's words, party battles "rouse the sluggish to exertion, give increased energy to the most active intellect, excite a salutary vigilance over our public functionaries, and prevent that apathy which has proved the ruin of Republics."

Apathy may indeed have proved the ruin of republics, but rousing the sluggish to exertion proved, ironically, the ruin of Van Buren. The architect of the party system became the first casualty of the razzle-dazzle campaigning the system quickly generated. The Whigs' Tippecanoe-and-Tyler-too campaign of 1840 transmuted the democratic Van Buren into a gilded aristocrat and assured his defeat at the polls. The "peddling for popularity" John Quincy Adams had deplored now became standard for party campaigners.

But the new methods were still forbidden to the presidential candidates themselves. The feeling lingered from earlier days that stumping the country in search of votes was demagoguery beneath the dignity of the presidency. Van Buren's code permitted—indeed expected—parties to inscribe their creed in platforms and candidates to declare their principles in letters published in newspapers. Occasionally candidates—William Henry Harrison in 1840, Winfield Scott in 1852—made a speech, but party surrogates did most of the hard work.

As late as 1858, Van Buren, advising his son John, one of the great popular orators of the time, on the best way to make it to the White House, emphasized the "rule . . . that the people will never make a man President who is so importunate as to show by his life and conversation that he not only has an eye on, but is in active pursuit of the office. . . . No man who has laid himself out for it, and was unwise enough to let the people into his secret, ever yet obtained it. Clay, Calhoun, Webster, Scott, and a host of lesser lights, should serve as a guide-post to future aspirants."

The continuing constraint on personal campaigning by candidates was reinforced by the desire of party managers to present their nominees as all things to all men. In 1835 Nicholas Biddle, the wealthy Philadelphian who had been Jackson's mortal opponent in the famous Bank War, advised the Whigs not to let General Harrison "say one single word about his principles or his creed. . . . Let him say nothing, promise nothing. Let no committee, no convention, no town meeting ever extract from him a single word about what he thinks now, or what he will do hereafter. Let the use of pen and ink be wholly forbidden as if he were a mad poet in Bedlam."

We cherish the memory of the famous debates in 1858 between Abraham Lincoln and Stephen A. Douglas. But those debates were not part of a presidential election. When the presidency was at stake two years later, Lincoln gave no campaign speeches on the issues darkly dividing the country. He even expressed doubt about party platforms—"the formal written platform system," as he called it. The candidate's character and record, Lincoln thought, should constitute his platform: "On just such platforms all our earlier and better Presidents were elected."

However, Douglas, Lincoln's leading opponent in 1860, foreshadowed the future when he broke the sound barrier and dared venture forth on thinly disguised campaign tours. Yet Douglas established no immediate precedent. Indeed, half a dozen years later Lincoln's successor, Andrew Johnson, discredited presidential stumping by his "swing around the circle" in the midterm election of 1866. "His performances in a western tour in advocacy of his own election," commented Benjamin F. Butler, who later led the fight in Congress for Johnson's impeachment, ". . . disgusted everybody." The tenth article of impeachment charged Johnson with bringing "the high office of the President of the United States into contempt, ridicule, and disgrace" by delivering "with a loud voice certain intemperate, inflammatory, and scandalous harangues . . . peculiarly indecent and unbecoming in the Chief Magistrate of the United States."

Though presidential candidates Horatio Seymour in 1868, Rutherford B. Hayes in 1876, and James A. Garfield in 1880 made occasional speeches, only Horace Greeley in 1872, James G. Blaine in 1884, and most spectacularly, William Jennings Bryan in 1896 followed Douglas's audacious example of stumping the country. Such tactics continued to provoke disapproval. Bryan, said John Hay, who had been Lincoln's private secretary and was soon to become McKinley's secretary of state, "is begging for the presidency as a tramp might beg for a pie."

Respectable opinion still preferred the "front porch" campaign, employed by Garfield, by Benjamin Harrison in 1888, and most notably by McKinley in 1896. Here candidates received and addressed numerous delegations at their own homes—a form, as the historian Gil Troy writes, of "stumping in place."

While candidates generally continued to stand on their dignity, popular campaigning in presidential elections flourished in these years, attaining new heights of participation (82 percent of eligible voters in 1876 and never once from 1860 to 1900 under 70 percent) and new wonders of pyrotechnics and ballyhoo. Parties mobilized the electorate as never before, and political iconography was never more ingenious and fantastic. "Politics, considered not as the science of government, but as the art of winning elections and securing office," wrote the keen British observer James Bryce, "has reached in the United States a development surpassing in elaborateness that of England or France as much as the methods of those countries surpass the methods of

Servia or Roumania." Bryce marveled at the "military discipline" of the parties, at "the demonstrations, the parades and receptions, the badges and brass bands and triumphal arches," at the excitement stirred by elections— and at "the disproportion that strikes a European between the merits of the presidential candidate and the blazing enthusiasm which he evokes."

Still the old taboo held back the presidential candidates themselves. Even so irrepressible a campaigner as President Theodore Roosevelt felt obliged to hold his tongue when he ran for reelection in 1904. This unwonted abstinence reminded him, he wrote in considerable frustration, of the July day in 1898 when he was "lying still under shell fire" during the Spanish-American War. "I have continually wished that I could be on the stump myself."

No such constraint inhibited TR, however, when he ran again for the presidency in 1912. Meanwhile, and for the first time, *both* candidates in 1908—Bryan again, and William Howard Taft—actively campaigned for the prize. The duties of the office, on top of the new requirements of campaigning, led Woodrow Wilson to reflect that same year, four years before he himself ran for President, "Men of ordinary physique and discretion cannot be Presidents and live, if the strain be not somehow relieved. We shall be obliged always to be picking our chief magistrates from among wise and prudent athletes,—a small class."

Theodore Roosevelt and Woodrow Wilson combined to legitimate a new conception of presidential candidates as active molders of public opinion in active pursuit of the highest office. Once in the White House, Wilson revived the custom, abandoned by Jefferson, of delivering annual state of the union addresses to Congress in person. In 1916 he became the first incumbent President to stump for his own reelection.

The activist candidate and the bully-pulpit presidency were expressions of the growing democratization of politics. New forms of communication were reconfiguring presidential campaigns. In the nineteenth century the press, far more fiercely partisan then than today, had been the main carrier of political information. In the twentieth century the spread of advertising techniques and the rise of the electronic media—radio, television, computerized public opinion polling—wrought drastic changes in the methodology of politics. In particular the electronic age diminished and now threatens to dissolve the historic role of the party.

The old system had three tiers: the politician at one end; the voter at the other; and the party in between. The party's function was to negotiate between the politician and the voters, interpreting each to the other and providing the link that held the political process together. The electric revolution has substantially abolished the sovereignty of the party. Where once the voter turned to the local party leader to find out whom to support, now he looks at television and makes up his own mind. Where once the politician turned to the local party leader to find out what people are thinking, he now takes a computerized poll.

The electronic era has created a new breed of professional consultants, "handlers," who by the 1980s had taken control of campaigns away from the politicians. The traditional pageantry—rallies, torchlight processions, volunteers, leaflets, billboards, bumper stickers—is now largely a thing of the past. Television replaces the party as the means of mobilizing the voter. And as the party is left to wither on the vine, the presidential candidate becomes more pivotal than ever. We shall see the rise of personalist movements, founded not on historic organizations but on compelling personalities, private fortunes, and popular frustrations. Without the stabilizing influence of parties, American politics would grow angrier, wilder, and more irresponsible.

Things have changed considerably from the austerities of the old republic. Where once voters preferred to call presumably reluctant candidates to the duties of the supreme magistracy and rejected pursuit of the office as evidence of dangerous ambition, now they expect candidates to come to them, explain their views and plead for their support. Where nonpartisan virtue had been the essence, now candidates must prove to voters that they have the requisite "fire in the belly." "'Twud be inth'restin," said Mr. Dooley, ". . . if th' fathers iv th' counthry cud come back an' see what has happened while they've been away. In times past whin ye voted f'r prisident ye didn't vote f'r a man. Ye voted f'r a kind iv a statue that ye'd put up in ye'er own mind on a marble pidistal. Ye nivir heerd iv George Wash'nton goin' around th' counthry distributin' five cint see-gars."

We have reversed the original notion that ambition must be disguised and the office seek the man. Now the man—and soon, one must hope, the woman— seeks the office and does so without guilt or shame or inhibition. This is not necessarily a degradation of democracy. Dropping the disguise is a gain for candor, and personal avowals of convictions and policies may elevate and educate the electorate.

On the other hand, the electronic era has dismally reduced both the intellectual content of campaigns and the attention span of audiences. In the nineteenth century political speeches lasted for a couple of hours and dealt with issues in systematic and exhaustive fashion. Voters drove wagons for miles to hear Webster and Clay, Bryan and Teddy Roosevelt, and felt cheated if the famous orator did not give them their money's worth. Then radio came along and cut political addresses down first to an hour, soon to thirty minutes—still enough time to develop substantive arguments.

But television has shrunk the political talk first to fifteen minutes, now to the sound bite and the thirty-second spot. Advertising agencies today sell candidates with all the cynical contrivance they previously devoted to selling detergents and mouthwash. The result is the debasement of American politics. "The idea that you can merchandise candidates for high office like breakfast cereal," Adlai Stevenson said in 1952, "is the ultimate indignity to the democratic process."

Still Bryce's "intermittent fever" will be upon us every fourth year. We will continue to watch wise if not always prudent athletes in their sprint for the White House, enjoy the quadrennial spectacle and agonize about the outcome.

"The strife of the election," said Lincoln after his reelection in 1864, "is but human-nature practically applied to the facts. What has occurred in this case, must ever recur in similar cases. Human-nature will not change."

Lincoln, as usual, was right. Despite the transformation in political methods there remains a basic continuity in political emotions. "For a long while before the appointed time has come," Tocqueville wrote more than a century and a half ago, "the election becomes the important and, so to speak, the all-engrossing topic of discussion. Factional ardor is redoubled, and all the artificial passions which the imagination can create in a happy and peaceful land are agitated and brought to light. . . .

"As the election draws near, the activity of intrigue and the agitation of the populace increase; the citizens are divided into hostile camps, each of which assumes the name of its favorite candidate; the whole nation glows with feverish excitement; the election is the daily theme of the press, the subject of every private conversation, the end of every thought and every action, the sole interest of the present.

"It is true," Tocqueville added, "that as soon as the choice is determined, this ardor is dispelled, calm returns, and the river, which had nearly broken its banks, sinks to its usual level; but who can refrain from astonishment that such a storm should have arisen?"

The election storm in the end blows fresh and clean. With the tragic exception of 1860, the American people have invariably accepted the result and given the victor their hopes and blessings. For all its flaws and follies, democracy abides.

Let us now turn the pages and watch the gaudy parade of American presidential politics pass by in all its careless glory.

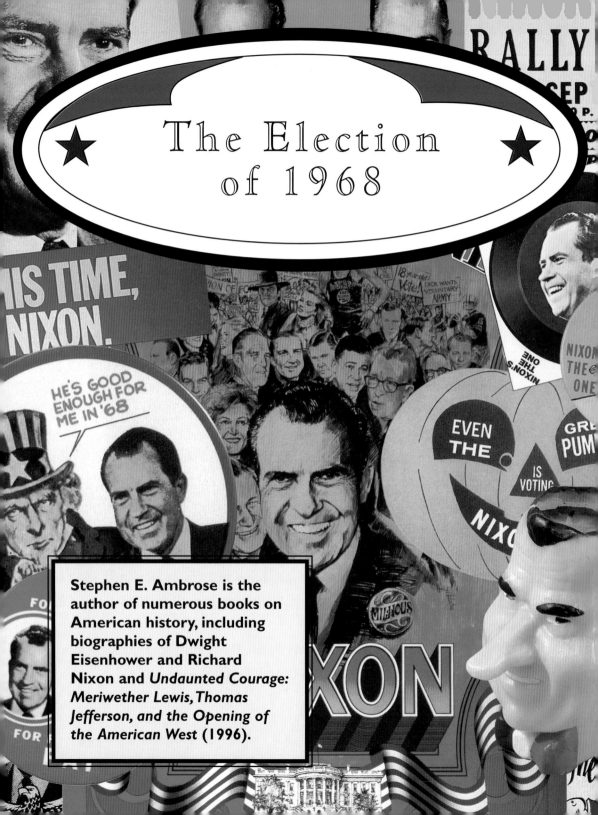

The Election of 1968

Stephen E. Ambrose is the author of numerous books on American history, including biographies of Dwight Eisenhower and Richard Nixon and *Undaunted Courage: Meriwether Lewis, Thomas Jefferson, and the Opening of the American West* (1996).

It was a tumultuous year, full of sharp surprises, shocking events, and fundamental changes in American society and politics. In January, victory in Vietnam seemed just around the corner; by November, the number of Americans killed in action was approaching 25,000 and victory seemed farther away than ever. At home, the generation gap, the gender gap, and the racial gap grew deeper and wider. Political assassinations sickened the nation; riots swept the country. Perhaps most surprising of all, President Lyndon Johnson dropped out of politics and Richard Nixon rose from his political grave to win the presidential election.

America's young people, especially on the college campuses, rejected the authority of their elders and the rules of their society. Some burned their draft cards, a few burned American flags, a handful openly called for a Communist victory in Vietnam. Widespread drug use became accepted, even common, as did rock-and-roll music, dirty blue jeans, long hair, and the slogan, "Don't trust anyone over thirty." American women embraced feminism in ever-increasing numbers. American blacks, many of them, rejected non-violence and took to the streets to demand equal rights or to call for "Black Power." In response to these and other developments, there was "backlash" by the white middle-class. The American people had not been so badly divided since the Civil War. As in 1861, in 1968 they split into two distinct groups: "doves" who opposed the war and embraced the social and political changes, and "hawks" who supported the war and traditional values.

The event that had the greatest impact on the presidential election came at the end of January on the other side of the world. The Communists in South Vietnam launched a country-wide offensive on the Vietnamese religious holiday of Tet. Although the offensive failed,

Eugene McCarthy became the hero of the "politics of protest," the hero of the new counterculture. Vietnam, the assassination of President Kennedy, the Mississippi Freedom Summer of 1964, police violence in the ghettos, and the murder of civil rights demonstrators contributed to the emergence of a protest movement—a dissenting generation.

it had a tremendous effect on the American people, who realized for the first time that they were not winning the war and that the Viet Cong were far more numerous and well-armed than anyone in power had ever indicated. The enemy inflicted heavy casualties on the American forces and stunned President Johnson. When his field commander, General William Westmoreland, asked for more than 200,000 reinforcements (at a time when he had more than 550,000 troops in country), Johnson knew that the American people would not support such an escalation and instead began, secretly, the long, slow process of withdrawal. His plan was to turn the war over to the South Vietnamese.

The almost certain Republican nominee, Richard Nixon, who had been calling for escalation for the previous four years, agreed with him—although he did not say so. Tet thus marked a turning point in world history; for the first time since 1898 the United States was reducing rather than increasing its armed forces in Asia.

The impact of Tet on the public was as great as its impact on American leaders, shown dramatically in the first presidential primary election, in March in New Hampshire. A little-known senator from Minnesota, Eugene McCarthy, challenged Johnson on an antiwar platform. He was given no chance, but he won 40 percent of the votes in the Democratic primary, which was interpreted as a defeat for Johnson and a rejection of his war policy. Four days after the primary Senator Robert Kennedy entered the contest for the Democratic nomination on an antiwar platform.

Two weeks later, on March 31, with the polls indicating that he was facing almost certain defeat in the upcoming Wisconsin primary, Johnson went on national television to make two surprise announcements. First, he

(Left) Plastic hat with paper hatband issued for the Democratic convention. Senator Eugene McCarthy ran in the Democratic primaries as an anti-Vietnam War candidate. (Right) Robert Kennedy Democratic convention hat. Sadly, Kennedy was assassinated on June 4, 1968, two months prior to the convention.

was halting nearly all bombing of North Vietnam and offering to enter into peace negotiations with the Communists. His previous position had been to demand a complete Communist withdrawal from South Vietnam. (Negotiations began in Paris in May and immediately stalled over the issue of South Vietnamese participation; the United States insisted on it, Hanoi refused to consider it.) Second, "I shall not seek, and I will not accept, the nomination of my party for another term as your President." The Democratic nomination was suddenly wide open. The three leading candidates were McCarthy, Kennedy, and Vice President Hubert Humphrey, who was pledged to continue the war and who counted on the party regulars rather than the votes of the people in the primaries for the nomination.

On April 4, another shock. Civil rights leader Martin Luther King Jr. was assassinated in Memphis. The murder led many young blacks to despair. A wave of riots swept the country. Parts of the nation's capital were in flames as buildings burned within blocks of the White House, Johnson brought 50,000 troops into Washington, D.C., to enforce a curfew and protect government property. Two weeks later another form of violence jolted the public, as young white students at

Humphrey's detractors insisted that he was a Johnson puppet, especially on the Vietnam War issue.

Auto license attachment for Wallace. George Wallace, former governor of Alabama, ran as a third-party candidate for president, endorsing segregation and conservative causes.

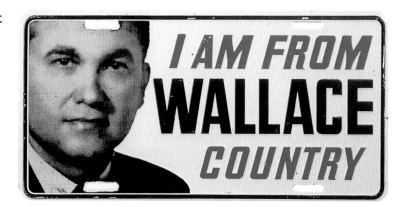

Columbia University seized administration buildings to protest both the war and black oppression. The Columbia radicals had many imitators. Campus violence erupted across the country.

The chief beneficiary of the backlash caused by the violence was Governor George Wallace of Alabama, who entered the race for the presidency as head of a third-party (the American Independent Party) ticket. His running mate was Air Force General Curtis LeMay, whose policy toward the enemy in Vietnam was to "bomb 'em back to the Stone Age." Wallace's slogan was, "Send Them a Message." He said that there wasn't a dime's worth of difference between the Republicans and the Democrats and attacked "pointy headed" intellectuals. He was anti-government, antiblack, antiviolence, and pro-war. The polls showed that he spoke for millions of angry Americans; they indicated that he was attracting more than 20 percent of the voters.

In the Democratic race, meanwhile, Kennedy was forging ahead. On June 5, he won a narrow victory over McCarthy in California that seemed to assure his nomination. But that night, at his victory celebration, he was assassinated by an Arab nationalist angry over his support of Israel. South Dakota Senator George McGovern, rather than Senator McCarthy, got the support of Kennedy's delegates, meaning that the doves in the party were split.

NIXON / AGNEW

cial Nixon Material – Feeley & Wheeler Inc., 370 Lexington Ave., New York, N.Y. 10017

Poster for Nixon and Agnew.

With the Democratic Party in turmoil, the Republicans met in early August in Miami to nominate Nixon. He had been campaigning, more or less nonstop, since his 1962 loss to Pat Brown in the California gubernatorial race, and had easily turned back the candidacies of Governors Nelson Rockefeller of New York and Ronald Reagan of California. Nixon picked Maryland Governor Spiro Agnew as his running mate. Agnew had propelled himself into national prominence in April with a get-tough policy toward black riots in Baltimore; his selection was an obvious attempt to persuade Wallace supporters not to throw away their vote on a third party but to get behind Nixon, who recognized that one of the chief battles in the November election would be for the traditionally Democratic white southern vote.

Nixon's platform was a moderate version of Wallace's; no busing for racial balance in the schools, an all-out attack on permissiveness, crime. and the Supreme Court's liberal decisions, and a restoration of family values and patriotism. All this was a part of what he called his "southern strategy." His slogan was "Nixon's the One!"

Boxed game on political strategy.

The 1968 presidential campaign raised concern over the viability of the U.S. political system. By the time the year had run its course, a sitting president announced he would not seek reelection; a presidential candidate and a prominent civil rights leader each had been murdered; and a national party convention was disrupted by riots and bloodshed.

HUBERT HUMPHREY MARCH

Eleanor Roosevelt said . . . "In him I see a spark of greatness!" Today, those who know him intimately, understand that here is a man fully qualified to lead this nation to new heights in self development and to once again regain the supremacy of respect throughout the world. He will be a Great President.

1968 was a year of trauma and tragedy in America. The limited amount and variety of Humphrey campaign items may be due to the lateness of the Democratic convention (August 26–29) and to the divisions within the party over the Vietnam War. The Republican campaign relied heavily on television, usually from studio sessions with a carefully screened audience.

On the number one issue, Nixon said he had a "plan to end the war and win the peace" but he gave no details (actually, his plan was the same as the policy Johnson had already—but still secretly, while denying it in public—initiated, the gradual withdrawal of American troops and the negotiation of a ceasefire). He had strong support from wealthy Americans, who put up enough money to give him the best financed campaign in American history to date. His campaign staff, headed by his law partner John Mitchell, was well-organized. In an innovation that became a permanent feature of presidential campaigning, he relied almost exclusively on television.

The emphasis on television was the idea of Nixon's chief of staff, H. R. "Bob" Haldeman. In a devastating critique of Nixon's 1960 campaign, Haldeman said that Nixon had spent too much time on the road, too much time making speeches. He wanted the candidate to make, at most, one speech per day. Television news programs would have to use a minute or two of it. Haldeman pointed out that the "sound bite," as it later came to be called, would reach more people in a day than three months of barnstorming.

Another Nixon innovation was to use professional advertising men rather than professional politicians as his principal advisers. Most of them came from the J. Walter Thompson advertising firm in Los Angeles. Frank Shakespeare, a CBS executive, was also on the staff. Nixon ignored the Republican National Committee and the party; he almost never used the word "Republican," nor did he campaign for Republican candidates.

The Democrats met in Chicago at the end of August. Their convention was a disaster. The

Humphrey celluloid button with moving eyes.

world watched aghast as the world's oldest political party tore itself apart. Inside the convention hall the delegates, tightly controlled by Johnson, nominated Hubert Humphrey, who had not won a single primary, and Senator Edmund Muskie. Outside the hall the Chicago police, stirred up and and encouraged by Mayor Richard Daley, went on a rampage against the youthful antiwar demonstrators, who for their part provoked the cops in every imaginable way.

The Democratic platform pledged to continue Johnson's policies in Vietnam. This left the doves without a candidate in the general election. This was dangerous not only to the Democratic Party, where the doves were a majority, but to democracy in America, as it left the doves feeling helpless, disillusioned, and frustrated. The number one political issue of 1968 was the war in Vietnam, but when the Democratic delegates turned back a "stop the bombing" resolution, the American people had no chance to vote on that number-one issue. This situation contributed heavily to the extreme bitterness of the presidential campaign. The only real winner from the Democratic convention was Richard Nixon, whose election now seemed assured—the polls indicated that he had a 43 percent to 31 percent lead over Humphrey (Wallace had 19 percent).

McCarthy poster by Ben Shahn.

Large plastic campaign buttons inspired by the *Laugh-In* television show.

When Humphrey began campaigning, he was greeted by hecklers chanting "Dump the Hump." It was a mark of how much the doves detested the Vietnam War that they forgot how much they detested Nixon. All three candidates were subjected to merciless heckling and disruptive tactics in their campaign appearances. Shouting matches replaced political discourse. Humphrey tried to reason with his hecklers; Wallace ridiculed and threatened his hecklers; Nixon's campaign staff screened out longhairs from his rallies or roughed them up.

Nixon took the high road, promising an end to the draft as soon as he had ended the war, the appointment of conservative strict constructionists to the Supreme Court, a balanced budget, and revenue sharing with the states (the federal money would presumably be used to lower state property taxes). In sharp contrast to his 1960 campaign, he scarcely mentioned foreign policy and refused to reveal his plan to end the war. He also refused Humphrey's demand for a debate, which led Humphrey to call him "Richard the Chickenhearted." Agnew took the low road, accusing Humphrey of being "squishy soft on Communism and soft on law and order."

Slowly, Humphrey began to cut into Nixon's lead, helped by the leaders of organized labor who could not stand Nixon and who were fearful of

Poster for Humphrey and Muskie associating them with John and Robert Kennedy and Martin Luther King Jr.

Wallace. Humphrey's greatest asset was that he was the candidate of the majority party, and he used it wisely. In sharpest possible contrast to Nixon, Humphrey consistently linked himself with his party. He worked closely with the Democratic National Committee Chairman Larry O'Brien. He mentioned Franklin Roosevelt, Harry Truman, John Kennedy, and even Johnson at every opportunity. He worked hard for Democratic congressional candidates.

Humphrey also helped himself by apparently putting some distance between his position and Johnson's (and Nixon's) on the war: toward the end of September, Humphrey declared that "it would be my policy to move toward systematic reduction in American forces. I think we can do it. I am determined to do it." Johnson was already doing it, but denying it; Nixon

Poster issued by the International Ladies Garment Workers Union promoting a series of campaign radio programs.

Campaign clothing items for Agnew and Humphrey.

planned to do it once elected, but denied it. The doves began, finally, to gather at the Humphrey roost. They flocked to it after September 30, when Humphrey came out for a bombing halt, saying he would take a "risk for peace."

Nixon fought back. He said the risk was not Humphrey's but the lives of American boys in Vietnam. He abandoned his promise to not indulge in "personal charges" and asserted that Humphrey had "a personal attitude of indulgence and permissiveness toward the lawless." Muskie, he said, was "giving aid and comfort to those who are tearing down respect for law across the country." In October, the Republicans ran a television commercial that showed battle scenes in Vietnam, black rioters in a burning American city, and a frail, starving child interspersed with scenes of Humphrey laughing and promoting "the politics of joy."

Wallace, meanwhile, was slipping, as third-party candidates traditionally do as election day approaches, By mid-October, he was down to 18 percent. Nixon was at 40 percent, Humphrey at 35 percent and moving up. It appeared all but certain that if Johnson declared a complete bombing halt and the beginning of serious peace negotiations, with President Nguyen Van Thieu's South Vietnamese government in Saigon

NIXON'S THE ONE!

Washington State Nixon for President—Gordon S. Clinton, Chairman

Automobile bumper sticker with Richard Nixon's most popular 1968 campaign slogan.

participating, Humphrey would forge ahead.

Anticipating that Johnson would do exactly that, Nixon moved to scuttle the peace prospects. "We do not want to play politics with peace," he declared as he began to do so. He made contact with Thieu through Mrs. Anna Chan Chennault, the Chinese widow of World War II hero General Claire Chennault. She had extensive contacts with the Saigon government. John Mitchell persuaded her to tell Thieu that if he refused to go to the peace table before the election, he could expect better treatment from a Republican administration.

On his own, Nixon attempted to undercut Johnson. On October 26 he praised Johnson for resisting pressure to contrive a "fake peace." But he said he had heard rumors about a bombing halt and charged that if true (he said they were), "this spurt of activity is a cynical, last-minute

The first team
VOTE
HUMPHREY-MUSKIE

AFL-CIO COPE, Washington, D.C. 20006

Poster for Humphrey and Muskie issued by the AFL-CIO.

Cardboard hanger for Humphrey.

attempt by President Johnson to salvage the candidacy of Mr. Humphrey." He then added he did not believe Johnson would do such a thing. But if the President did halt the bombing, Nixon went on, it would constitute a "thinly disguised surrender."

Hanoi got into action. On October 27 the Communists agreed to respect the de-militarized zone separating North and South Vietnam, and to allow Saigon to sit at the negotiating table in return for a bombing halt. Johnson, meanwhile, was pressuring Thieu to accept a bombing halt in return for a place at the peace table, but Thieu refused. Desperate, Johnson decided to go ahead without Saigon. On October 31 he announced that he had ordered a bombing halt and that the expanded peace talks would get started on November 6, the day after the election.

A wave of relief swept across the nation. Polls conducted on November 1 showed a 55–28 approval for the bombing halt. Humphrey made it clear that "an enormous burden had been lifted from his candidacy." Even as Humphrey passed him in the polls, Nixon let the euphoria build, counting on Thieu to sabotage the peace talks. On November 2, Humphrey went ahead of Nixon, 43 percent to 40 percent (Wallace was down to 13 percent).

But that same day Thieu announced that his government "deeply regrets not being able to participate in the peace talks."

Now Nixon went into action. In his memoirs, he admitted that "I wanted to plant the impression . . . that [Johnson's] motives and his timing" were political. His aides charged that Johnson had instituted the bombing halt as a ploy in the election. In a television interview, Nixon said "many people . . . seem to share that view . . . because the pause came so late in the campaign." He added that one of his aides felt that the halt "was politically motivated and was timed to affect the election. I don't agree with him, but he is a man in his own right and has made this statement." Then he offered to help persuade Saigon to sit down at the negotiation table after he won the election.

On Monday, November 4, in a nationwide telethon, Nixon pounded home the point that "the high hopes for peace of three days ago" had dwindled. He said he would not criticize Johnson's motives, "but when we consider the fact that hopes for peace . . . are quite discouraging because of the developments [since the bombing halt announcement] it is clear that if we are going to avoid what could be a diplomatic disaster, it is going to be necessary to get some new men and a united front in the United States." Then he said he had heard "a very disturbing report" that since the bombing halt went into effect, "the North Vietnamese are moving thousands of tons of supplies down the Ho Chi Minh Trail, and our bombers are not able to stop them."

He had heard no such report.

Cardboard Halloween-related campaign item.

He simply made that up. Humphrey, on his own telethon, made that point and added, "It does not help the negotiations to falsely accuse anyone at this particular time."

Agnew was not present for the Nixon telethon. He had become an embarrassment to the Republicans (a Democratic radio spot opened with a soft, steady "thump, thump." Then, above the thumping, a voice asked incredulously: "Spiro Agnew? A heartbeat away from the presidency?" The Democrats had used a somewhat similar negative adver-

Labor union sticker for Humphrey-Muskie.

Property of Dexter Middle School Library

tisement against Barry Goldwater in 1964; a trend was being established). On the Democratic telethon, Muskie got equal billing with Humphrey, who declared, "My co-pilot, Ed Muskie, is ready to take over at any time." Humphrey's praise of Muskie became so effusive that one reporter composed a make-believe lead for his election day story that read, "Vice President Hubert H. Humphrey pledged today that if elected, he will resign immediately and let Senator Edmund S. Muskie become President."

The election was one of the closest in American history. As the votes were counted first Nixon, then Humphrey had slight leads. Not until noon the following day was Nixon declared the winner. He had won 31,770,000 votes (43.4 percent) to Humphrey's 31,270,000 (42.7 percent). Wallace got 9,906,000 (13.5 percent). In the electoral college, however, Nixon had a solid victory, 301 votes to Humphrey's 191 and Wallace's 46. Nixon had carried all the Great Plains states and the Far West (except Washington

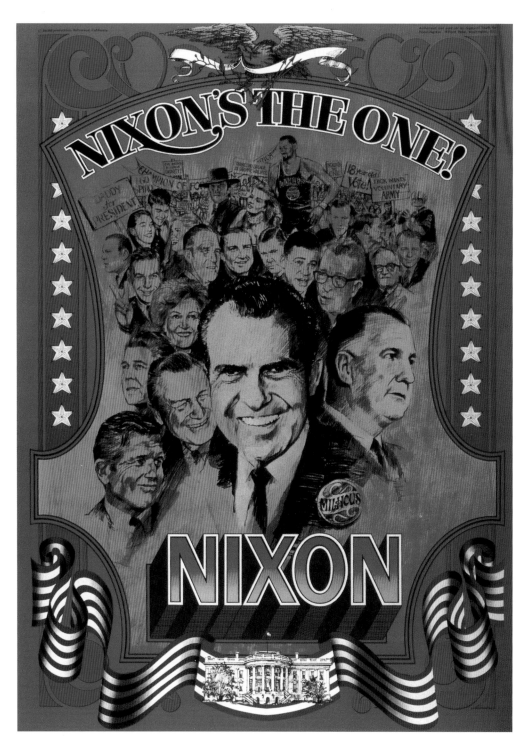

state); Humphrey had carried most of the Northeast; Nixon won the Middle West six states to two (Minnesota and Michigan); Humphrey won Texas; Nixon got Florida, South Carolina and the border states; Wallace won Arkansas, Louisiana, Mississippi, Alabama, and Georgia.

Nixon was the first candidate since Zachary Taylor in 1848 to win the presidency while his party failed to carry either the House or Senate (the Democrats had a majority of 58–42 in the Senate, 243–192 in the House).

The campaign had been characterized by lies, deceit, and cynical contempt by the politicians, and by hostility, anger, disruptive tactics by the people. Campaigns are supposed to divide the people into "them" and "us," but within the confines of a recognition that they are all Americans, one people living together in one country.

In his victory speech on November 6, Nixon spoke to the problem the campaign had created for him. He said he had seen many placards during the campaign, some friendly, some not. "But the one that touched me the most was the one that I saw in Deshler, Ohio, at the end of a long day. . . . A teenager held up a sign, 'Bring Us Together.'

"And that will be the great objective of this administration at the outset, to bring the American people together."

The people very badly needed to be brought back together after the most divisive presidential campaign since 1860. Less clear was whether Nixon was the man who could do it. His campaign had capitalized on the polarization among the people. The tactic had worked. But now he had to govern, and his campaign had so badly divided the already badly divided nation that it was going to be at best difficult for him to do so.

(Opposite) The most widely circulated poster of the 1968 campaign. Perhaps every American college dormitory had one on a wall—either to show support or to throw darts at.

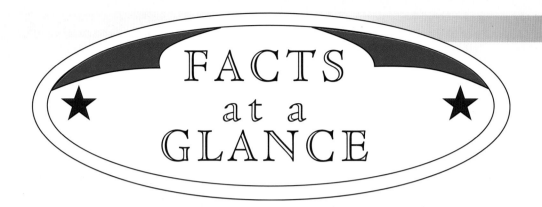

FACTS at a GLANCE

RICHARD M. NIXON

- **Born:** January 9, 1913, in Yorba Linda, California
- **Parents:** Francis and Hannah Milhous Nixon
- **Education:** Graduated from Whittier College (1934) and Duke University Law School (1937)
- **Occupation:** lawyer, politician
- **Married:** Thelma "Patricia" Catherina Ryan (1912–1993) on June 21, 1940.
- **Children:** Patricia Nixon (1946–   ); Julie Nixon (1948–   )
- **Died:** April 22, 1994, in New York City

Served as the 37TH PRESIDENT OF THE UNITED STATES,

- January 20, 1969, to August 9, 1974

VICE PRESIDENT

- Spiro T. Agnew (1969–73)
- Gerald Ford (1973–74)

OTHER POLITICAL POSITIONS

- Attorney for U.S. Office of Emergency Management, 1942
- Member of U.S. House of Representatives, 1947–51
- United States Senator, 1951–53
- Vice President, 1953–61

CABINET

Secretary of State
- William P. Rogers (1969–73)
- Henry A. Kissinger (1973–74)

Secretary of the Treasury
- David M. Kennedy (1969–70)
- John B. Connally, Jr. (1971–72)
- George P. Shultz (1972–74)
- William E. Simon (1974)

Secretary of Defense
- Melvin R. Laird (1969–72)
- Elliot L. Richardson (1973)
- James R. Schlesinger (1973–74)

Attorney General
- John N. Mitchell (1969–72)
- Richard G. Kleindienst (1972–73)
- Elliot L. Richardson (1973)
- William B. Saxbe (1974)

Postmaster General
- Winton M. Blount (1969–71)

Secretary of the Interior
- Walter J. Hickel (1969–70)
- Rogers C. B. Morton (1971–74)

Secretary of Agriculture
- Clifford M. Hardin (1969–71)
- Earl L. Butz (1971–74)

Secretary of Commerce
- Maurice H. Stans (1969–72)
- Peter G. Peterson (1972)
- Frederick B. Dent (1973–74)

Secretary of Labor
- George P. Schultz (1969–70)
- James D. Hodgson (1970–72)
- Peter J. Brennan (1973–74)

Secretary of Health, Education, and Welfare
- Robert H. Finch (1969–70)
- Elliot L. Richardson (1970–73)
- Caspar W. Weinberger (1973–74)

Secretary of Housing and Urban Development
- George W. Romney (1969–72)
- James T. Lynn (1973–74)

Secretary of Transportation
- John A. Volpe (1969–73)
- Claude S. Brinegar (1973–74)

NOTABLE EVENTS DURING NIXON'S ADMINISTRATION

1969   Richard Nixon is inaugurated as the 37th president.

1970   In April, U.S. troops sent to Cambodia; on May 1, four students at an antiwar protest at Kent State University are shot and killed by members of the National Guard; in July Nixon proposes the establishment of the Environmental Protection Agency.

1971   On June 10, Nixon lifts the U.S. trade embargo with communist China; the *New York Times* begins publishing the secret "Pentagon Papers," which provide a history of U.S. involvement in Vietnam; in August, Nixon becomes the first president to establish peacetime price and wage controls.

1972   Meets with Chinese Premier Chou En-Lai in Peking; period of *détente* begins with the signing of the Strategic Arms Limitation Treaty (SALT I) with the Soviet Union in May; on June 17, five burglars are arrested breaking into the Democratic Party head-quarters at the Watergate office complex in Washington, D.C.; in August, U.S. combat troops are withdrawn from Vietnam; in November Nixon is reelected president by a wide margin.

1973   In February the Senate establishes a special committee to investigate Watergate; Spiro Agnew resigns on October 14.

1974   Nixon refuses the Watergate Committee subpoena to turn over recordings of White House conversations; the House of Representatives Judiciary Committee opens impeachment hearings on May 9; Nixon resigns as president on August 9, and Vice President Gerald Ford is sworn in as the 38th president of the United States; in September, Ford pardons Nixon for any crimes he may have committed while in office.

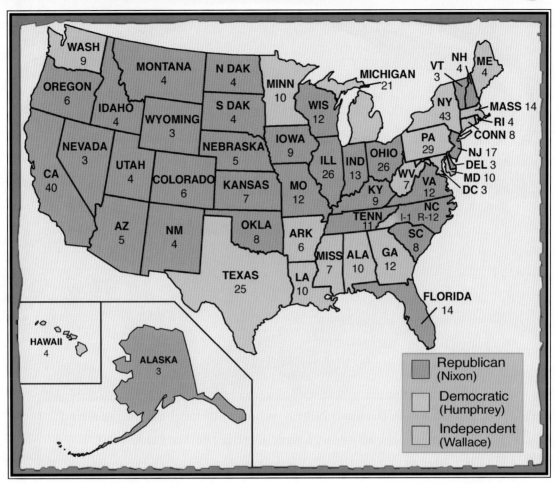

In the 1968 Presidential election, Richard Nixon received 43.4 percent of the popular vote, the lowest for a winning candidate since Woodrow Wilson in the three-way election of 1912. Of the 13 states in the once solid Democratic South, Hubert Humphrey carried only Texas. Five southern states went to George Wallace and seven to Nixon. Nixon had a solid majority in the electoral college, with 301 votes to 191 for Humphrey and 46 for Wallace.

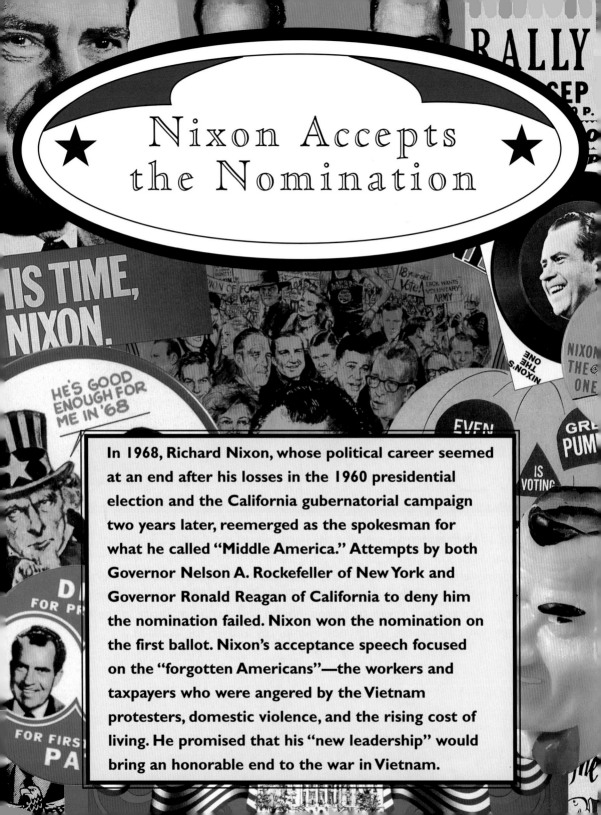

Nixon Accepts the Nomination

In 1968, Richard Nixon, whose political career seemed at an end after his losses in the 1960 presidential election and the California gubernatorial campaign two years later, reemerged as the spokesman for what he called "Middle America." Attempts by both Governor Nelson A. Rockefeller of New York and Governor Ronald Reagan of California to deny him the nomination failed. Nixon won the nomination on the first ballot. Nixon's acceptance speech focused on the "forgotten Americans"—the workers and taxpayers who were angered by the Vietnam protesters, domestic violence, and the rising cost of living. He promised that his "new leadership" would bring an honorable end to the war in Vietnam.

Sixteen years ago I stood before this convention to accept your nomination as the running mate of one of the greatest Americans of our time or any time—Dwight D. Eisenhower.

Eight years ago I had the highest honor of accepting your nomination for President of the United States.

Tonight I again proudly accept that nomination for President of the United States.

But I have news for you. This time there's a difference—this time we're going to win.

We're going to win for a number of reasons. First a personal one.

General Eisenhower, as you know, lies critically ill in the Walter Reed Hospital tonight. I have talked, however, with Mrs. Eisenhower on the telephone.

She tells me that his heart is with us. She says that there is nothing that he lives more for, and there is nothing that would lift him more than for us to win in November.

And I say let's win this one for Ike.

We're going to win because this great convention has demonstrated to the nation that the Republican Party has the leadership, the platform, and the purpose that America needs.

We're going to win because you have nominated as my running mate a statesman of the first rank who will be a great campaigner, and one who is fully qualified to undertake the new responsibilities that I shall give to the next Vice President of the United States.

And he is a man who fully shares my conviction and yours that after a period of 40 years when power has gone from the cities and the states to the Government in Washington, D.C., it's time to have power go back from Washington to the states and to the cities of this country all over America.

DICK NIXON — *The One Man to Deal With Khrushchev*

Nixon items from his 1960 campaign for the presidency. Nixon lost a close election to John F. Kennedy; two years later, after losing the race for governor of California, he indicated that he was ending his political career. Instead, he began working to regain the Republican Party's presidential nomination, succeeding in 1968.

We're going to win because at a time that America cries out for the unity that this Administration has destroyed, the Republican Party, after a spirited contest for its nomination for President and Vice President, stands united before the nation tonight.

And I congratulate Governor Reagan, I congratulate Governor Rockefeller, I congratulate Governor Romney, I congratulate all those who have made the hard fight that they have for this nomination, and I know that you will all fight even harder for the great victory our party is going to win in November because we're going to be together in that election campaign.

And a party that can unite itself will unite America.

My fellow Americans, most important we're going to win because our cause is right. We make history tonight not for ourselves but for the ages. The choice we make in 1968 will determine not only the future of America but the future of peace and freedom in the world for the last third of the 20th century, and the question that we answer tonight: can America meet this great challenge?

Let us listen to America to find the answer to that question.

As we look at America, we see cities enveloped in smoke and flame. We hear sirens in the night. We see Americans dying on distant battlefields abroad. We see Americans hating each other; fighting each other; killing each other at home.

And as we see and hear these things, millions of Americans cry out in anguish: Did we come all this way for this? Did American boys die in Normandy and Korea and in Valley Forge for this?

Listen to the answers to those questions.

It is another voice, it is a quiet voice in the tumult of the shouting. It is the voice of the great majority of Americans, the forgotten Americans, the non shouters, the non demonstrators. They're not racists or sick; they're not guilty of the crime that plagues the land; they are black, they are white; they're native born and foreign born; they're young and they're old.

They work in American factories, they run American businesses. They serve in government; they provide most of the soldiers who die to keep it free. They give drive to the spirit of America. They give lift to the American dream. They give steel to the backbone of America.

They're good people. They're decent people; they work and they save and they pay their taxes and they care.

Like Theodore Roosevelt, they know that this country will not be a good place for any of us to live in unless it's a good place for all of us to live in.

And this I say, this I say to you tonight, is the real voice of America. In this year 1968, this is the message it will broadcast to America and to the world.

Let's never forget that despite her faults, America is a great nation. And America is great because her people are great.

With Winston Churchill we say, we have not journeyed all this way, across the centuries, across the oceans, across the mountains, across the prairies because we are made of sugar candy.

America's in trouble today not because her people have failed but because her leaders have failed. And what America wants are leaders to match the greatness of her people.

And this great group of Americans—the forgotten Americans and others—know that the great question Americans must answer by their votes in November is this: Whether we will continue for four more years the policies of the last five years.

And this is their answer, and this is my answer to that question: When the strongest nation in the world can be tied up for four years in a war in Vietnam with no end in sight, when the richest nation in the world can't manage its own economy, when the nation with the greatest tradition of the rule of law is plagued by unprecedented lawlessness, when a nation that has been known for a century for equality of opportunity is torn by unprecedented racial violence, and when the President of the United States cannot travel abroad or to any major city at home without fear of a hostile demonstration—then it's time for new leadership for the United States of America.

Thank you. My fellow Americans, tonight I accept the challenge and the commitment to provide that new leadership for America and I ask you to accept it with me.

And let us accept this challenge not as a grim duty but as an exciting adventure in which we are privileged to help a great nation realize its destiny and let us begin by committing ourselves to the truth, to see it like it is and tell it like it is, to tell the truth, to speak the truth, and to live the truth. That's what we will do.

We've had enough of big promises and little action. The time has come for an honest government in the United States of America.

And so tonight I do not promise the millennium in the morning. I don't promise that we can eradicate poverty and end discrimination and eliminate all danger of wars in the space of four or even eight years. But I do promise action. A new policy for peace abroad, a new policy for peace and progress at home.

Look at our problems abroad. Do you realize that we face the stark truth that we are worse off in every area of the world tonight than we were when President Eisenhower left office eight years ago? That's the record.

And there is only one answer to such a record of failure, and that is the complete house cleaning of those responsible for the failures and that record. The answer is the complete reappraisal of America's policy in every section of the world. We shall begin with Vietnam.

We all hope in this room that there's a chance that current negotiations may bring an honorable end to that war. And we will say nothing during this campaign that might destroy that chance.

And if the war is not ended when the people choose in November, the choice will be clear. Here it is: For four years this administration has had at its disposal the greatest military and economic advantage that one nation has ever had over another in a war in history. For four years America's fighting men have set a record for courage and sacrifice unsurpassed in our history. For four years this Administration has had the support of the loyal opposition for the objective of seeking an honorable end to the struggle.

Never has so much military and economic and diplomatic power been used so ineffectively. And if after all of this time, and all of this sacrifice, and all of this support, there is still no end in sight, then I say the time has come for the American people to turn to new leadership not tied to the mistakes and policies of the past. That is what we offer to America.

And I pledge to you tonight that the first priority foreign policy objective of our next Administration will be to bring an honorable end to the war in Vietnam. We shall not stop there. We need a policy to prevent more Vietnams. All of America's peacekeeping institutions and all of America's foreign commitments must be reappraisal.

Over the past 25 years, America has provided more than $150 billion in foreign aid to nations abroad. In Korea, and now again in Vietnam, the United States furnished most of the money, most of the arms, most of the men to help the people of those countries defend themselves against aggression. Now we're a rich country, we're a strong nation, we're a populous nation but there are 200 million Americans and there are two billion people that live in the free world, and I say the time has come for other nations in the free world to bear their fair share of the burden of defending peace and freedom around this world.

What I call for is not a new isolationism. It is a new internationalism in which America enlists its allies and its friends around the world in those struggles in which their interest is as great as ours.

And now to the leaders of the Communist world we say, after an era of confrontations, the time has come for an era of negotiations.

Where the world super-powers are concerned there is no acceptable alternative to peaceful negotiation. Because this will be a period of negotiations we shall restore the strength of America so that we shall always negotiate from strength and never from weakness.

And as we seek through negotiations let our goals be made clear. We do not seek domination over any other country. We believe deeply in our ideas but we believe they should travel on their own power and not on the power of our arms. We shall never be belligerent. But we shall be as firm in defending our system as they are in expanding theirs.

We believe this should be an era of peaceful competition not only in the productivity of our factories but in the quality of our ideas. We extend the hand of friendship to all people. To the Russian people. To the Chinese people. To all people in the world. And we shall work toward the goal of an open world,

Campaign record for Nixon with excerpts from his acceptance speech, August 8, 1968.

open sky, open cities, open hearts, open minds. The next eight years my friends—this period in which we're entering—I think we will have the greatest opportunity for world peace, but also face the greatest danger of world war of any time in our history.

I believe we must have peace. I believe that we can have peace. But I do not underestimate the difficulty of this task.

Because, you see, the art of preserving peace is greater than that of waging war, and much more demanding.

But I am proud to have served in an Administration which ended one war and kept the nation out of other wars for eight years afterward.

And it is that kind of experience, and it is that kind of leadership, that America needs today and that we will give to America, with your help.

And as we commit the new policies for America tonight, let me make one further pledge. For five years hardly a day has gone by when we haven't read or heard a report of the American flag being spit on, and our embassy being stoned, a library being burned, or an ambassador being insulted some place in the world, and each incident reduced respect for the United States until the ultimate insult inevitably occurred.

And I say to you tonight that when respect for the United States of America falls so low that a fourth-rate military power like Korea will seize an American naval vessel in the high seas, it's time for new leadership to restore respect for the United States of America.

Thank you very much. My friends, America is a great nation. It is time we started to act like a great nation around the world.

It's ironic to note, when we were a small nation, weak militarily and poor economically, America was respected. And the reason was that America stood for something more powerful than military strength or economic wealth.

The American Revolution was a shining example of freedom in action which caught the imagination of the world, and today, too often, America is an example to be avoided and not followed.

A nation that can't keep the peace at home won't be trusted to keep the peace abroad. A President who isn't treated with respect at home will not be treated with respect abroad. A nation which can't manage its own economy can't tell others how to manage theirs.

If we are to restore prestige and respect for America abroad, the place to begin is at home—in the United States of America.

My friends, we live in an age of revolution in America and in the world. And to find the answers to our problems, let us turn to a revolution—a revolution that will never grow old, the world's greatest continuing revolution, the American Revolution.

The American Revolution was and is dedicated to progress. But our founders recognized that the first requisite of progress is order.

Now there is no quarrel between progress and order because neither can exist without the other.

So let us have order in America, not the order that suppresses dissent and discourages change but the order which guarantees the right to dissent and provides the basis for peaceful change.

And tonight it's time for some honest talk about the problem of order in the United States. Let us always respect, as I do, our courts and those who serve on them, but let us also recognize that some of our courts in their decisions have gone too far in weakening the peace forces as against the criminal forces in this country.

Let those who have the responsibility to enforce our laws, and our judges who have the responsibility to interpret them, be dedicated to the great principles of civil rights. But let them also recognize that the first civil right of every American is to be free from domestic violence. And that right must be guaranteed in this country.

And if we are to restore order and respect for law in this country, there's one place we're going to begin: We're going to have a new Attorney General of the United States of America.

I pledge to you that our new Attorney General will be directed by the President of the United States to launch a war against organized crime in this country.

I pledge to you that the new Attorney General of the United States will be an active belligerent against the loan sharks and the numbers racketeers that rob the urban poor in our cities.

I pledge to you that the new Attorney General will open a new front against the pill peddlers and the narcotics peddlers who are corrupting the lives of the children of this country.

Because, my friends, let this message come through clear from what I say tonight. Time is running out for the merchants of crime and corruption in American society. The wave of crime is not going to be the wave of the future in the United States of America.

We shall reestablish freedom from fear in America so that America can take the lead of reestablishing freedom from fear in the world.

And to those who say that law and order is the code word for racism, here is a reply: Our goal is justice—justice for every American. If we are to have respect for law in America, we must have laws that deserve respect. Just as we cannot have progress without order, we cannot have order without progress.

And so as we commit to order tonight, let us commit to progress.

And this brings me to the clearest choice among the great issues of this campaign.

For the past five years we have been deluged by Government programs for the unemployed, programs for the cities, programs for the poor, and we have reaped from these programs an ugly harvest of frustrations, violence and failure across the land. And now our opponents will be offering more of the same—more billions for Government jobs, Government housing, Government welfare. I say it's time to quit pouring billions of dollars into programs that have failed in the United States of America.

To put it bluntly, we're on the wrong road and it's time to take a new road to progress.

Again we turn to the American Revolution for our answers. The war on poverty didn't begin five years ago in this country, it began when this country began.

It's been the most successful war on poverty in the history of nations. There's more wealth in America today, more broadly shared than in any nation in the world.

We are a great nation. And we must never forget how we became great.

America is a great nation today, not because of what government did for people, but because of what people did for themselves over 190 years in this country.

And so it is time to apply the lessons of the American Revolution to our present problems.

Let us increase the wealth of America so we can provide more generously for the aged and for the needy and for all those who cannot help themselves.

But for those who are able to help themselves, what we need are not more millions on welfare rolls but more millions on payrolls in the United States of America.

Instead of Government jobs and Government housing and Government welfare, let Government use its tax and credit policies to enlist in this battle the greatest engine of progress ever developed in the history of man— American private enterprise.

Let us enlist in this great cause the millions of Americans in volunteer organizations who will bring a dedication to this task that no amount of money can ever buy.

And let us build bridges, my friends, build bridges to human dignity across that gulf that separates black America from white America.

Black Americans—no more than white Americans—do not want more Government programs which perpetuate dependency. They don't want to be a colony in a nation. They want the pride and the self-respect and the dignity that can only come if they have an equal chance to own their own homes, to own their own businesses, to be managers and executives as well as workers, to have a piece of the action in the exciting ventures of private enterprise.

I pledge to you tonight that we shall have new programs which will provide that equal chance. We make great history tonight. We do not fire a shot heard round the world, but we shall light the lamp of hope in millions of homes across this world in which there is no hope today.

And that great light shining out from America will again become a beacon of hope for all those in the world who seek freedom and opportunity.

My fellow Americans, I believe that historians will recall that 1968 marked the beginning of the American generation in world history. Just to be alive in America, just to be alive at this time is an experience unparalleled in history. Here's where the nation is.

Think: Thirty-two years from now most of the Americans living today will celebrate a New Year that comes once in a thousand years.

Eight years from now, in the second term of the next President, we will celebrate the 200th anniversary of the American Revolution.

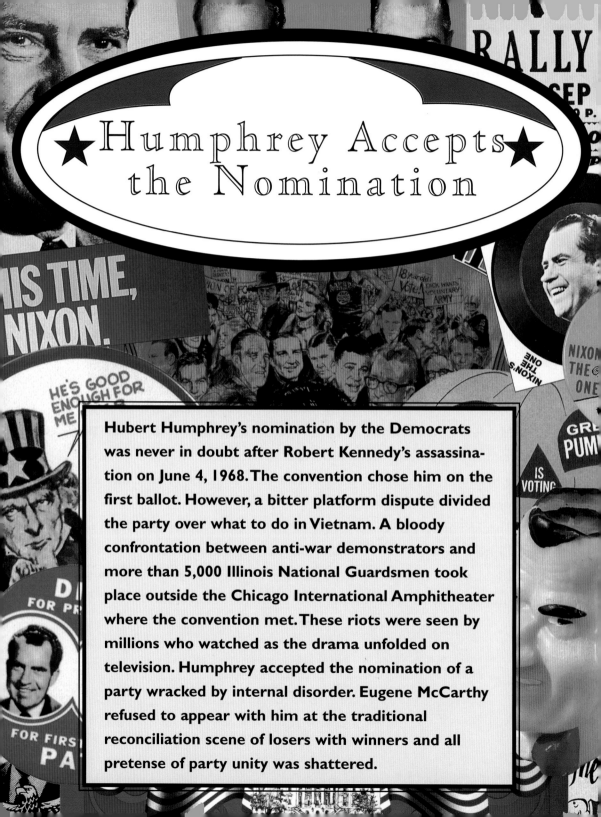

★Humphrey Accepts★ the Nomination

Hubert Humphrey's nomination by the Democrats was never in doubt after Robert Kennedy's assassination on June 4, 1968. The convention chose him on the first ballot. However, a bitter platform dispute divided the party over what to do in Vietnam. A bloody confrontation between anti-war demonstrators and more than 5,000 Illinois National Guardsmen took place outside the Chicago International Amphitheater where the convention met. These riots were seen by millions who watched as the drama unfolded on television. Humphrey accepted the nomination of a party wracked by internal disorder. Eugene McCarthy refused to appear with him at the traditional reconciliation scene of losers with winners and all pretense of party unity was shattered.

Mr. Chairman, my fellow Americans, my fellow Democrats—I proudly accept the nomination of our party.

This moment—this moment is one of personal pride and gratification. Yet one cannot help but reflect the deep sadness that we feel over the troubles and the violence which have erupted, regrettably and tragically, in the streets of this great city, and for the personal injuries which have occurred.

Surely we have now learned the lesson that violence breeds counter-violence and it cannot be condoned, whatever the source.

I know that every delegate to this convention shares tonight my sorrow and my distress over these incidents. And for just one moment, in sober reflection and serious purpose, may we just quietly and silently, each in our own way, pray for our country. And may we just share for a moment a few of those immortal words of the prayer of St. Francis of Assisi, words which I think may help heal the wounds, ease the pain and lift our hearts.

Listen to this immortal saint: "Where there is hatred, let me know love. Where there is injury, pardon. Where there is doubt, faith. Where there is despair, hope. Where there is darkness, light."

Those are the words of a saint. And may those of us of less purity listen to them well and may America tonight resolve that never, never again shall we see what we have seen.

Yes, I accept your nomination in this spirit and I have spoken knowing that the months and the years ahead will severely test our America. And might I say that as this America is tested, that once again we give our testament to America. And I do not think it is sentimental nor is it cheap, but I think it is true that each and everyone of us in our own way should once again affirm to ourselves and our posterity that we love this nation, we love America!

But take heart my fellow Americans. This is not the first time that our nation has faced a challenge to its life and its purpose. And each time that we've had to face these challenges we have emerged with new greatness and with new strength.

We must make this moment of crisis a moment of creation.

As it has been said, in the worst of times a great people must do the best of things—and let us do it. We stand at such a moment now in the affairs of this Nation, because, my fellow Americans, something new, something different has happened. There is an end of an era, and there is the beginning of a new day.

And it is the special genius of the Democratic Party that it welcomes change—not as an enemy but as an ally—not as a force to be suppressed but as an instrument of progress to be encouraged.

This week our party has debated the great issues before America in this very hall, and had we not raised these issues—troublesome as they were—we would have just ignored the reality of change.

Had we just papered over the differences of frank, hard debate, we would deserve the contempt of our fellow citizens and the condemnation of history.

Yes, we dare to speak out and we have heard hard and sometimes bitter debate. But I submit that this is the debate, and this is the work of a free people, the work of an open convention and the work of a political party responsive to the needs of this nation.

Democracy affords debate, discussion, and dissent. But, my fellow Americans, it also requires decision. And we have decided here, not by edict, but by vote; not by force, but by ballot.

Majority rule has prevailed but minority rights are preserved.

There is always the temptation, always the temptation to leave the scene of battle in anger and despair, but those who know the true meaning of democracy accept the decision of today but never relinquishing their right to change it tomorrow.

Cartoon-type campaign buttons. Humphrey was the son of a South Dakota druggist.

In the space of but a week this convention has literally made the foundations of a new Democratic Party structure in America. From precinct level to the floor of this convention, we have revolutionized our rules and procedures.

And that revolution is in the proud tradition of our party. It is in the tradition of Franklin Roosevelt, who knew that America had nothing to fear but fear itself!

And it is in the tradition of that one and only Harry Truman, who let 'em have it and told it like it was.

And that's the way we're going to do it from here on out.

And it is in the tradition of that beloved man, Adlai Stevenson, who talked sense to the American people—and oh, tonight, how we miss this great, good, and gentle man of peace in America—

And my fellow Americans, all that we do and all that we ever hope to do, must be in the tradition of John F. Kennedy, who said to us: Ask not what your country can do for you, but what you can do for your country.

And, my fellow Democrats and fellow Americans, in that spirit of that great man let us ask what together we can do for the freedom of man.

And what we are doing is in the tradition of Lyndon B. Johnson, who rallied a grief-stricken nation when our leader was stricken by the assassin's bullet and said to you and said to me, and said to all the world—let us continue.

Celluloid button for Humphrey from Minnesota, his home state.

And in the space, and in the space of five years since that tragic moment, President Johnson has accomplished more of the unfinished business of America than any of his modern predecessors.

And I truly believe that history will surely record the greatness of his contribution to the people of this land.

And tonight to you, Mr. President, I say thank you. Thank you, Mr. President.

Yes, my fellow Democrats, we have recognized and indeed we must recognize the end of an era and the beginning of a new day—and that new day belongs to the people—to all the people, everywhere in this land of the people, to every man, woman and child that is a citizen of this Republic.

And within that new day lies nothing less than the promise seen a generation ago by that poet Thomas Wolfe—to every man his chance, to every man regardless of his birth his shining golden opportunity, to every man the right to live and to work and to be himself, and to become whatever thing his manhood and his vision can combine to make him—this is the promise of America.

Yes, the new day is here across America. Throughout the entire world forces of emancipation are at work. We hear freedom's rising chorus—"Let me live my own life, let me live in peace, let me be free," say the people.

And that cry is heard today in our slums, on our farms, and in our cities. It is heard from the old as well as from the young. It is heard in Eastern Europe and it is heard in Vietnam. And it will be answered by us, in how we face the three realities that confront this nation.

The first reality is the necessity for peace in Vietnam and in the world.

The second reality, the second reality is the necessity for peace and justice in our cities and our nation.

And the third reality is the paramount necessity for unity—unity in our country.

Let me speak first, then, about Vietnam.

There are differences of course, serious differences within our party on this vexing and painful issue of Vietnam, and these differences are found even within the ranks of all the Democratic Presidential candidates.

But I might say to my fellow Americans that once you have examined the differences I hope you will also recognize the much larger areas of agreement.

Let those who believe that our cause in Vietnam has been right, or those who believe that it has been wrong, agree here and now, that neither vindication nor repudiation will bring peace or be worthy of this country!

The question is not the yesterdays but the question is what do we do now? No one knows what the situation in Vietnam will be when the next President of the United States takes that oath of office on January 20, 1969.

But every heart in America prays that by then we shall have reached a cease-fire in all Vietnam and be in serious negotiation toward a durable peace.

Meanwhile, as a citizen, a candidate, and Vice President, I pledge to you and to my fellow Americans that I will do everything within my power, within the limits of my capacity and ability to aid the negotiations and to bring a prompt end to this war!

May I remind you of the words of a truly great citizen of the world, Winston Churchill. It was he who said—and we should heed his words well—"those who use today and the present to stand in judgment of the past may well lose the future."

And if there is any one lesson that we should have learned, it is the policies of tomorrow need not be limited by the policies of yesterday.

My fellow Americans, if it becomes my high honor to serve as President of these states and people, I shall apply that lesson to the search for peace in Vietnam as to all other areas of national policy. [. . .]

Now our second reality is the necessity for peace at home. There is, my friends—let's see it as it is—there is trouble in America. But it does not come from a lack of faith. But it comes from the kindling of hope.

When the homeless can find a home, they do not give up the search for a better home. When the hopeless find hope, they seek higher hopes. And in 1960 and again in 1964, you, the American people, gave us a mandate to awaken America. You asked us to get America moving again, and we have—and America is on the move.

And we have, we have awakened expectations. We have aroused new voices and new voices that must and will be heard.

We have inspired new hope in millions of men and women, and they are impatient—and rightfully so, impatient now to see their hopes and their aspirations fulfilled.

We have raised a new standard of life in our America, not just for the poor but for every American—wage earner, businessman, farmer, school child, and housewife. A standard by which the future progress must be judged.

Our most urgent challenge is in urban America, where most of our people live. Some 70 percent of our people live on 2 percent of our land, and within 25 years 100 million more will join our national family.

I ask you tonight—where shall they live? How shall they live? What shall be their future? We're going to decide in the next four years those questions. The next President of the United States will establish policies not only for this generation but for children yet unborn. Our task is tremendous and I need your help.

The simple solution of the frustrated and frightened to our complex urban problems is to lash out against society. But we know—and they must know—that this is no answer.

Violence breeds more violence: disorder destroys, and only in order can we build. Riot makes for ruin; reason makes for solution. So from the White House to the courthouse to the city hall, every official has the solemn respon-

Paper sticker for Humphrey.

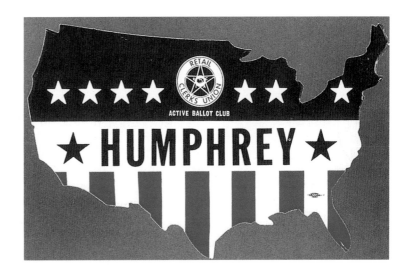

sibility of guaranteeing to every American—black and white, rich and poor—the right to personal security—life.

Every American, black or white, rich or poor, has the right in this land of ours to a safe and decent neighborhood, and on this there can be no compromise.

I put it very bluntly—rioting, burning, sniping, mugging, traffic in narcotics, and disregard for law are the advance guard of anarchy, and they must and they will be stopped.

But may I say most respectfully, particularly to some who have spoken before, the answer lies in reasoned, effective action by state, local, and Federal authority. The answer does not lie in an attack on our courts, our laws, or our Attorney General.

We do not want a police state. But we need a state of law and order.

We do not want a police state but we need a state of law and order, and neither mob violence nor police brutality have any place in America.

And I pledge to use every resource that is available to the Presidency, every resource available to the President, to end once and for all the fear that is in our cities.

Celluloid button for McCarthy reflecting his opposition to the Vietnam War.

Now let me speak of other rights. Nor can there be any compromise with the right of every American who is able and who is willing to work to have a job—that's an American right, too.

Who is willing to be a good neighbor, to be able to live in a decent home in the neighborhood of his own choice.

Nor can there be any compromise with the right of every American who is anxious and willing to learn, to have a good education.

And it is to these rights—the rights of law and order, the rights of life, the rights of liberty, the right of a job, the right of a home in a decent neighborhood, and the right of an education—it is to these rights that I pledge my life and whatever capacity and ability I have.

And now the third reality, essential if the other two are to be achieved, is the necessity, my fellow Americans, for unity in our country, for tolerance and forbearance and for holding together as a family, and we must make a great decision. Are we to be one nation, or are we to be a nation divided, divided between black and white, between rich and poor, between north and south, between young and old? I take my stand—we are and we must be one nation, united by liberty and justice for all, one nation under God, indivisible with liberty and justice for all. This is our America.

Just as I said to you there can be no compromise on the right of personal security, there can be no compromise on securing of human rights. [. . .]

And now I appeal, I appeal to those thousands—yea millions—of young Americans to join us, not simply as campaigners, but to continue as vocal, creative and even critical participants in the politics of our time. Never were you needed so much, and never could you do so much if you want to help now.

Martin Luther King Jr. had a dream. Robert F. Kennedy as you saw

Lithographed tin button for Robert Kennedy.

tonight had a great vision. If Americans will respond to that dream and that vision, their deaths will not mark the moment when America lost its way. But it will mark the time when America found its conscience.

These men, these men have given us inspiration and direction, and I pledge from this platform tonight we shall not abandon their purpose—we shall honor their dreams by our deeds now in the days to come.

I am keenly aware of the fears and frustrations of the world in which we live. It is all too easy, isn't it, to play on these emotions. But I do not intend to do so. I do not intend to appeal to fear, but rather to hope. I do not intend to appeal to frustration, but rather to your faith.

I shall appeal to reason and to your good judgment.

The American Presidency, the American Presidency is a great and powerful office, but it is not all-powerful. It depends most of all upon the will and the faith and the dedication and the wisdom of the American people.

So I call you forth—I call forth that basic goodness that is there—I call you to risk the hard path of greatness.

And I say to America. Put aside recrimination and dissension. Turn away from violence and hatred. Believe—believe in what America can do, and believe in what America can be, and with the vast—with the help of that vast, unfrightened, dedicated, faithful majority of Americans. I say to this great convention tonight, and to this great nation of ours, I am ready to lead our country!

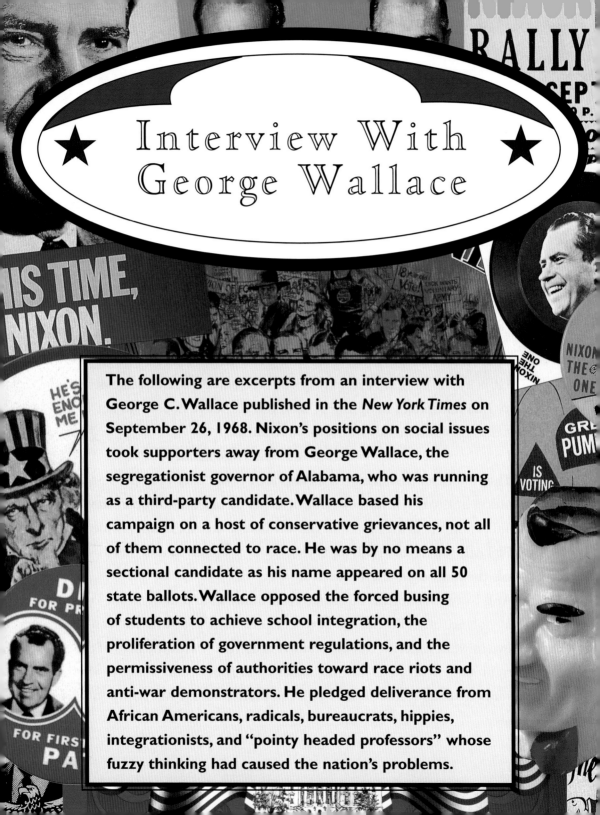

Interview With George Wallace

The following are excerpts from an interview with George C. Wallace published in the *New York Times* on September 26, 1968. Nixon's positions on social issues took supporters away from George Wallace, the segregationist governor of Alabama, who was running as a third-party candidate. Wallace based his campaign on a host of conservative grievances, not all of them connected to race. He was by no means a sectional candidate as his name appeared on all 50 state ballots. Wallace opposed the forced busing of students to achieve school integration, the proliferation of government regulations, and the permissiveness of authorities toward race riots and anti-war demonstrators. He pledged deliverance from African Americans, radicals, bureaucrats, hippies, integrationists, and "pointy headed professors" whose fuzzy thinking had caused the nation's problems.

Question: We have a Constitution that's served in the country over a great many years, and now we have got lots of new problems and things of that kind. Do you think the Constitution is as good today as it was when it was written or does it need some updating, an amendment or something?

Answer: The Constitution of the country is still just as good a document as it was when written, as far as I'm concerned. It has provisos for amendment process.

Q. Right.

A. And I can think of at least one amendment that ought to be submitted to the people of the country; submitted to the legislatures, rather. And that's the one involving the public school system.

Q. What would that be, Governor?

A. It would be an amendment declaring that absolute control of the public school systems should vest in the states, and all matters involving privileges and immunities and the due process of law that arose thereunder, insofar as was the law, in my judgment, prior to the takeover of the public school system by the Federal courts and the Federal Government. By usurpation of authority, the judges nullified the Tenth Amendment.

Q. This would be, in essence, an amendment that would revoke the 1954 [school desegregation] decision of the Court?

A. Well, not necessarily—the 1954 decision was an anti-discrimination decision. I don't know that anybody argues with an anti-discrimination decision. In the long run, of course, what the argument was about was that they knew and we knew that this was not just anti-discrimination and we were correct. It was a matter of forceful take-over, and forced compliance with whatever guidelines are written by the Federal Government. They have jumped from non-discrimination to complete control.

For instance, we had freedom of choice in the public school system in

Alabama and Texas and the other states of this region, but the Federal authorities filed a suit in which they said not enough people chose to go to the proper schools.

That showed that they were not truthful when they said they believed in this decision; they really didn't believe in this decision unless it did what they wanted it to do.

And so the free choice proposition of being able to choose to go to any school you want to go to regardless of race didn't work, and bring about those changes that the pseudo-intellectuals, the smart folks, the people that want to handle my child's life and tell me what to do with my child, and what neighborhood for him to go to school wished. It didn't work. That is, the people didn't choose like they thought they would choose.

And so now they say you must choose for them, and if you don't choose for them, then we are going to choose for them. And so, in Alabama, for instance, they just arbitrarily ordered the closing down of 100 schools, including some new multimillion-dollar high schools—just closed them down.

Q. We have a war in Vietnam today, and we never have declared war. I wonder why we don't do that?

A. I think the really important thing is that we are in Vietnam with a half million American servicemen whose lives are at stake and who are totally committed, whether we agree with the war or not. As long as they are there we must do whatever is necessary for their interest. That is what I am concerned about.

My main concern is the safety for those who are being shot at. Now, I was shot at during the war, and I know how it feels to be shot at. I think our main concern is their safety and health at the present time. And then you bring up the matter of aiding the Communists, why that's one reason this movement has strong support as all these pseudo-intellectual definitions of treason and academic freedom run counter to the common sense judgment of the average man.

While his sons are over there being shot at by the Communists, and his grandsons, you can let somebody go out and raise money and blood and fly the flag of the people trying to kill his son. And you let a professor make a speech that's reprinted in the Communist capitals saying, we wish defeat for our servicemen. And the theoreticians say [in Washington] we can't do anything about that because we haven't really declared war.

Q. Would you do something different?

A. Many people at the time questioned our moral position in World War II. But we got into it. I am glad we defeated the Nazis and Fascists. When we got into it we saw it to a conclusion. I think that we ought to have a reappraisal of our position with our allies, telling them that it is as much your interest as it is ours, that you have as much at stake as we do, and we expect you to help us.

Now, we can't make them help us. But we can think about our commitments, all the way from military to money, and we can think about what they owe us. I believe that since they need us and we need them, that they would respect us more and we would get more support for our position if we laid it on the line with them.

Q. I also think that you had something on your mind about Vietnam that you wanted to say, and we got off that subject.

A. Well, we talked about our involvement there and about our allies, and of course, like I say in my speeches, I hope and pray the peace talks in Paris are successful, and I believe if we could have an honorable peace through negotiations, that's best. Hopefully, diplomacy and political negotiations will settle the war honorably and peaceably and bring the servicemen home, but it looks like the Paris talks may fail.

Q. Do you have some pattern in your mind about that settlement?

A. Well, of course, I don't think that settlement ought to be one in which we just completely surrender the South Vietnamese Government to the Vietcong and a coalition government really, in the long run, amounts to that.

If we fail in getting a guarantee of the integrity of South Vietnam, then I think that we are going to have to turn to the Joint Chiefs of Staff for advice and if they feel that a military conclusion through the use of conventional weapons can be brought up—that is, a military victory—then I would be for that.

Q. There's the question of the nuclear antiproliferation treaty that has come up in the campaign. Mr. Nixon says he's for it, but he thinks we ought to delay making any moves for ratification of it. Mr. Humphrey is on the other side. Do you have any particular views about that?

A. Well, of course, I think it would be good to stop the proliferation of nuclear weapons. But, of course, the signing of a treaty doesn't necessarily mean the Communists will abide by the treaty, because they will proliferate, if they want to, and nonproliferate, if they don't want to proliferate.

So I think that any agreement we make with them in this field, or any other field, ought to be one providing for adequate inspection programs.

I just don't believe the Communists on their word, and I don't think you folks do either. But I think we should wait awhile on the ratification of the treaty, but with the understanding that we are still interested in nonproliferation of nuclear weapons.

In view of the recent actions of the Communists in Czechoslovakia I think perhaps it's good to delay it. But we should never say that we are going to forget about proliferation. I think we ought to stop the proliferation of atomic nuclear devices.

Q. Why not go ahead and sign it now?

A. Well, maybe in that way we can let the Russians know we are not pleased with their actions in Europe.

Q. What about the Supreme Court, Governor? You are talking about the Supreme Court and the decisions. Would you have any program dealing with the Supreme Court?

A. Yes, I'd sponsor a mountain climbing expedition for some of them to

Automobile license attachments for Wallace. Wallace found it difficult to outdo the determination of Nixon and Agnew to bring "law and order" to the country.

draw off some of their excess energy. However, attrition takes its toll under every Administration. And I would appoint people differently oriented in the first place.

In the second place, I would ask that Congress provide, through Constitutional amendment or otherwise, whichever is appropriate, that the term be limited to, say, eight years, and that they then have to be reconfirmed by the Senate of the United States. I'd also recommend an age limit, a retirement time.

Q. Governor, you have said a couple of times here, in discussing the strength of your movement and your chances for election, that one of the reasons you stand a good chance is because the people are angry and they are mad for a whole series of reasons. Is there a danger that that anger could fall over into actual violence?

A. No sir. Some of you folks—I don't mean you, personally, but I am talking about your paper and other papers—you sympathize with and help build up the forces who believe in violence because you have written editorials declaring what a great movement it was to lie down in the streets. Those are the people that have brought about the anarchy and violence in the country. Unless that is contained and controlled, you are going to have a movement that's not going to be on the left. It's going to be on the other side and it's going to stop all of this.

That's the fear, that's one reason I am running for President. I want to change some things in the country—within the constitutional context—at the ballot box and thus prevent violence.

We are not going out here and ask that a hundred thousand people march in Raleigh, N.C., that a hundred thousand march in Montgomery, Ala., or here in Dallas, or Houston. You have been with us and seen the crowds we had. We don't ask them to do that. We say "You must obey the law and obey court orders, whether you like them or not."

You see, this is for the purpose of preventing what we are talking about and it is to stop this group of militants and anarchists from threatening the mass of people in the country. When you go to hear me speak and there are 200 in Milwaukee [anti-Wallace demonstrators] there with Father [James] Groppi and 7,000 inside and that many more on the

Caricature candle of Nixon.

outside supporting us, you understand how they are outnumbered in the nation as far as people are concerned. Those people that were applauding me outnumber this group.

We must control this group of militants and anarchists from threatening the mass of people in the country. Unless we stop their activities, I mean, their unlawful activities, they are going to be in danger themselves.

Q. But, is the only solution to this beating them on the head?

A. We have tried every other solution. The previous administrations have passed every civil rights bill known to man to placate the anarchists, including the open housing bill. Senator Robert Kennedy said when he was living, "Let's just pass these bills and get people out of the streets into the courts."

And the more bills they passed and laws and judgments they rendered, the more activity we had in the streets. So we have spent billions of dollars in the poverty program to give people money, and you still have street mobs, so what else do you suggest?

Q. What do you suggest?

A. In France they were about to destroy the republic as a result of revolution in the street. What did de Gaulle say the last time? "This is the last of it," didn't he say? "We are going to suppress it next time with whatever suppression is necessary." Well, you haven't had any more of it, have you? Why not try that? The idea of people throwing bombs and looting and burning and laughing and carrying on while the police are ordered to stand around and watch them doesn't make sense.

Q. Do you think this represents the large percentage of the population?

A. No, I think it represents a small percentage of the population. I think the majority of black and white people are overwhelmingly against it, and want it stopped. It is a few folks who take advantage of the situation—a few militants.

Prior to this, if you had any mob action, the same newspapers who now say go soft on those rioters and looters said "Shoot those folks." Now, it is turned

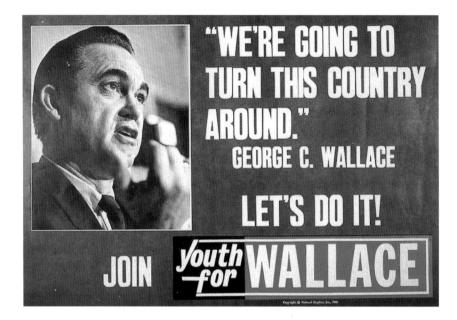

Poster for
Wallace.

around the other way, and then you want to handle looters and arsonists with kid gloves.

Maybe that is the way folks at the *New York Times* think it ought to be done, but the masses of people are tired of it. The man who goes out and works 25 years for a home, works every day and then his home is burned down, he is mad! He can't walk in his neighborhood in most cities of the United States at night without fear of something happening to him.

And the policeman who makes any effort to do anything about this crime often ends up being sued, demoted, fired, or suspended.

People are tired of this, and there is a way to stop it. Proper use of the police power is the only thing left now to try to curtail anarchy in the country. Everything else has failed.

Q. May I ask you another question, a direct question? Are you a segregationist?

A. Well, what do you mean by a segregationist?

Q. Do you believe in segregation?

A. Well, segregation of the races? In what respect?

Q. Schools and hospitals?

A. In the first place, you are asking me a question about something that never has existed in the history of the country. We have never had what your definition of segregation is, to exist in the South. In fact, we have had more mixing and mingling and togetherness and association there than you have had in New York City, where the *New York Times* is located. We have worked together, we have sat together, we have ridden together, we have been completely together in the South.

We did have in the school system a separation because the schools in the rural South were the social center. And we did have social separation as you have in New York, and as you have in your family life. And so we just had a common sense social separation—the schools were the social center. But if you mean complete separation of the races, we have never had that and I hope we never will have it.

Q. But do you advocate a return to segregation of the schools?

A. No sir. I do not advocate that.

Q. In Alabama?

A. No, sir. I don't advocate that. I am running for the Presidency of the United States on the platform of turning the control of the public school systems back to the people of the states. And I would say that you would not have a completely segregated system in Alabama.

But, you would have a control of the system that would mean it would never deteriorate to such a status as the Washington school system, and some of the schools in New York City have deteriorated into. God help us if our schools ever get to be a jungle like you have some in New York City, and like you have in Washington, and like you have in Philadelphia—

Q. Well, the reason—

A. They can't even play high school football games before crowds. In Philadelphia they play football games behind locked gates with just the cheerleaders—no spectators, because they had a race riot at every football game. I think schools should be controlled locally.

Q. The reason I asked the question is that I wondered if you have changed your views?

A. No, sir, I haven't changed my views at all. I said I thought the segregated school system was the best school system in Alabama. It was a system that had peace and tranquility. And after all, there is something to say for peace and tranquility.

Although the theoreticians and the newspapers and others think it is not so important to have a peaceful and tranquil community and a peaceful and tranquil school system. It is a real good school system compared to some they have in some parts of the country. So a segregated system has been the best school system for Alabama, that is correct.

Q. Well, do you think—?

Nixon was heavily favored in the 1968 election. He promised to heed the "quiet voice of the great majority of Americans . . . the non-shooters, the non-demonstrators." He made it into an "us versus them" contest, the "us" being middle America—the white, middle-class, patriotic "forgotten Americans."

Nixon won 32 states with 301 electoral votes. In the popular vote, Nixon received 43.4 percent. A white backlash did take place, validating Nixon's strategy. Of the 13 states in the once solid Democratic South, Humphrey carried only Texas. While 95 percent of black voters cast their ballot for Humphrey, less than 35 percent of whites did so. Three out of ten white Johnson voters in 1964 cast their vote for either Nixon or Wallace in 1968. In his memoirs, Nixon stressed that 57 percent of the voters had voted for either him or Wallace, meaning that a majority favored a change. However, the type of change wanted by the American people remained unclear.

A. I am running for the Presidency of the United States, and I want to leave it to the states. And so I would make no recommendation to Alabama.

Q. To the states or to local school boards?

A. Well, to the states, as every local school board is a creature of the states and the states created—all political subdivisions—so leave it to the states. The states have, by enactment of their legislatures, given authority to local school boards to administer school affairs in their particular localities.

The reason local school boards have control of schools in Alabama is because the State of Alabama, the sovereign, granted no authority to the states. So when you leave it to the States, you are leaving it, in effect, to the local school boards.

Q. Do you think blacks and whites, they just ordinarily want to stab one another?

A. Want to do what?

Q. Want to stab one another.

A. I didn't say that they want to stab one another. I just said that in your school systems and parts of the country you have fights and friction and violence every week.

Q. Well, what does that have to do with segregation and integration, now?

A. Forced mixing in the big school systems at an abnormal rate has brought violence in the school systems, that's correct.

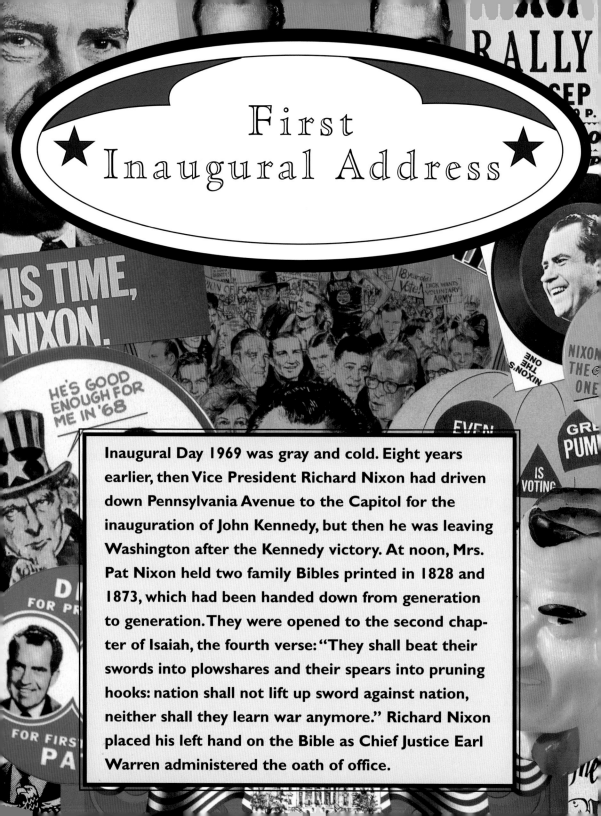

First Inaugural Address

Inaugural Day 1969 was gray and cold. Eight years earlier, then Vice President Richard Nixon had driven down Pennsylvania Avenue to the Capitol for the inauguration of John Kennedy, but then he was leaving Washington after the Kennedy victory. At noon, Mrs. Pat Nixon held two family Bibles printed in 1828 and 1873, which had been handed down from generation to generation. They were opened to the second chapter of Isaiah, the fourth verse: "They shall beat their swords into plowshares and their spears into pruning hooks: nation shall not lift up sword against nation, neither shall they learn war anymore." Richard Nixon placed his left hand on the Bible as Chief Justice Earl Warren administered the oath of office.

I ask you to share with me today the majesty of this moment. In the orderly transfer of power, we celebrate the unity that keeps us free.

Each moment in history is a fleeting time, precious and unique. But some stand out as moments of beginning, in which courses are set that shape decades or centuries.

This can be such a moment.

Forces now are converging that make possible, for the first time, the hope that many of man's deepest aspirations can at last be realized. The spiraling pace of change allows us to contemplate, within our own lifetime, advances that once would have taken centuries.

In throwing wide the horizons of space, we have discovered new horizons on earth.

For the first time, because the people of the world want peace, and the leaders of the world are afraid of war, the times are on the side of peace.

Eight years from now America will celebrate its 200th anniversary as a nation. Within the lifetime of most people now living, mankind will celebrate that great new year which comes only once in a thousand years—the beginning of the third millennium.

What kind of nation we will be, what kind of world we will live in, whether we shape the future in the image of our hopes, is ours to determine by our actions and our choices.

The greatest honor history can bestow is the title of peacemaker. This honor now beckons America—the chance to help lead the world at last out of the valley of turmoil, and onto that high ground of peace that man has dreamed of since the dawn of civilization.

If we succeed, generations to come will say of us now living that we mastered our moment, that we helped make the world safe for mankind.

This is our summons to greatness.

I believe the American people are ready to answer this call.

The second third of this century has been a time of proud achievement. We have made enormous strides in science and industry and agriculture. We have shared our wealth more broadly than ever. We have learned at last to manage a modern economy to assure its continued growth.

We have given freedom new reach, and we have begun to make its promise real for black as well as for white.

We see the hope of tomorrow in the youth of today. I know America's youth. I believe in them. We can be proud that they are better educated, more committed, more passionately driven by conscience than any generation in our history.

No people has ever been so close to the achievement of a just and abundant society, or so possessed of the will to achieve it. Because our strengths are so great, we can afford to appraise our weaknesses with candor and to approach them with hope.

Standing in this same place a third of a century ago, Franklin Delano Roosevelt addressed a Nation ravaged by depression and gripped in fear. He could say in surveying the Nation's troubles: "They concern, thank God, only material things."

Our crisis today is the reverse.

We have found ourselves rich in goods, but ragged in spirit; reaching with magnificent precision for the moon, but falling into raucous discord on earth.

We are caught in war, wanting peace. We are torn by division, wanting unity. We see around us empty lives, wanting fulfillment. We see tasks that need doing, waiting for hands to do them.

To a crisis of the spirit, we need an answer of the spirit.

To find that answer, we need only look within ourselves. When we listen to "the better angels of our nature," we find that they celebrate the simple things, the basic things—such as goodness, decency, love, kindness.

Greatness comes in simple trappings.

The simple things are the ones most needed today if we are to surmount what divides us, and cement what unites us.

ATTEND
NIXON
RALLY
SAT. SEPT. 21
➤ at 3:00 P. M. ◄
LEVITTOWN
SHOP - A - RAMA
RT. 13 & LEVITTOWN PKW.
AND THEN VOTE FOR
NIXON - AGNEW
➤ on NOV. 5th, 1968 ◄
Paid for by: United Citizens for NIXON - AGNEW, Bucks County Republican Committee

A variety of ephemera from Nixon's 1968 campaign is pictured here, as well as on the following pages.

THIS TIME, NIXON.

To lower our voices would be a simple thing.

In these difficult years, America has suffered from a fever of words; from inflated rhetoric that promises more than it can deliver; from angry rhetoric that fans discontents into hatreds; from bombastic rhetoric that postures instead of persuading.

We cannot learn from one another until we stop shouting at one another—until we speak quietly enough so that our words can be heard as well as our voices.

For its part, government will listen. We will strive to listen in new ways—to the voices of quiet anguish, the voices that speak without words, the voices of the heart—to the injured voices, the anxious voices, the voices that have despaired of being heard.

Those who have been left out, we will try to bring in.

Those left behind, we will help to catch up.

For all of our people, we will set as our goal the decent order that makes progress possible and our lives secure.

As we reach toward our hopes, our task is to build on what has gone before—not turning away from the old, but turning toward the new.

In this past third of a century, government has passed more laws, spent more money, initiated more programs, than in all our previous history.

In pursuing our goals of full employment, better housing, excellence in education; in rebuilding our cities and improving our rural areas; in protecting our environment and enhancing the quality of life—in all these and more, we will and must press urgently forward.

We shall plan now for the day when our wealth can be transferred from the destruction of war abroad to the urgent needs of our people at home.

The American dream does not come to those who fall asleep.

But we are approaching the limits of what government alone can do.

Our greatest need now is to reach beyond government, and to enlist the legions of the concerned and the committed.

What has to be done, has to be done by government and people together or it will not be done at all. The lesson of past agony is that without the people we can do nothing; with the people we can do everything.

To match the magnitude of our tasks, we need the energies of our people—enlisted not only in grand enterprises, but more importantly in those small, splendid efforts that make headlines in the neighborhood newspaper instead of the national journal.

With these, we can build a great cathedral of the spirit—each of us raising it one stone at a time, as he reaches out to his neighbor, helping, caring, doing.

I do not offer a life of uninspiring ease. I do not call for a life of grim sacrifice. I ask you to join in a high adventure—one as rich as humanity itself, and as exciting as the times we live in.

The essence of freedom is that each of us shares in the shaping of his own destiny.

Until he has been part of a cause larger than himself, no man is truly whole.

The way to fulfillment is in the use of our talents; we achieve nobility in the spirit that inspires that use.

As we measure what can be done, we shall promise only what we know we can produce, but as we chart our goals we shall be lifted by our dreams.

No man can be fully free while his neighbor is not. To go forward at all is to go forward together.

This means black and white together, as one nation, not two. The laws have caught up with our conscience. What remains is to give life to what is in the law: to ensure at last that as all are born equal in dignity before God, all are born equal in dignity before man.

As we learn to go forward together at home, let us also seek to go forward together with all mankind.

Let us take as our goal: where peace is unknown, make it welcome; where peace is fragile, make it strong; where peace is temporary, make it permanent.

After a period of confrontation, we are entering an era of negotiation.

Let all nations know that during this administration our lines of communication will be open.

We seek an open world—open to ideas, open to the exchange of goods and people—a world in which no people, great or small, will live in angry isolation.

We cannot expect to make everyone our friend, but we can try to make no one our enemy.

Those who would be our adversaries, we invite to a peaceful competition—

not in conquering territory or extending dominion, but in enriching the life of man.

As we explore the reaches of space, let us go to the new worlds together—not as new worlds to be conquered, but as a new adventure to be shared.

With those who are willing to join, let us cooperate to reduce the burden of arms, to strengthen the structure of peace, to lift up the poor and the hungry.

But to all those who would be tempted by weakness, let us leave no doubt that we will be as strong as we need to be for as long as we need to be.

Over the past twenty years, since I first came to this Capital as a freshman Congressman, I have visited most of the nations of the world.

I have come to know the leaders of the world, and the great forces, the hatreds, the fears that divide the world.

I know that peace does not come through wishing for it—that there is no substitute for days and even years of patient and prolonged diplomacy.

I also know the people of the world.

I have seen the hunger of a homeless child, the pain of a man wounded in battle, the grief of a mother who has lost her son. I know these have no ideology, no race.

I know America. I know the heart of America is good.

I speak from my own heart, and the heart of my country, the deep concern we have for those who suffer, and those who sorrow.

I have taken an oath today in the presence of God and my countrymen to uphold and defend the Constitution of the United States. To that oath I now add this sacred commitment: I shall consecrate my office, my energies, and all the wisdom I can summon, to the cause of peace among nations.

Let this message be heard by strong and weak alike:

The peace we seek to win is not victory over any other people, but the peace that comes "with healing in its wings"; with compassion for those who have suffered; with understanding for those who have opposed us; with the opportunity for all the peoples of this earth to choose their own destiny.

Only a few short weeks ago, we shared the glory of man's first sight of the world as God sees it, as a single sphere reflecting light in the darkness.

As the Apollo astronauts flew over the moon's gray surface on Christmas Eve, they spoke to us of the beauty of earth—and in that voice so clear across the lunar distance, we heard them invoke God's blessing on its goodness.

In that moment, their view from the moon moved poet Archibald MacLeish to write:

"To see the earth as it truly is, small and blue and beautiful in that eternal silence where it floats, is to see ourselves as riders on the earth together, brothers on that bright loveliness in the eternal cold—brothers who know now they are truly brothers."

In that moment of surpassing technological triumph, men turned their thoughts toward home and humanity—seeing in that far perspective that man's destiny on earth is not divisible; telling us that however far we reach into the cosmos, our destiny lies not in the stars but on Earth itself, in our own hands, in our own hearts.

We have endured a long night of the American spirit. But as our eyes catch the dimness of the first rays of dawn, let us not curse the remaining dark. Let us gather the light.

Our destiny offers, not the cup of despair, but the chalice of opportunity. So let us seize it, not in fear, but in gladness—and, "riders on the earth together," let us go forward, firm in our faith, steadfast in our purpose, cautious of the dangers; but sustained by our confidence in the will of God and the promise of man.

The Invasion of Cambodia

On April 20, 1970, President Nixon announced that Vietnamization and the phased withdrawal of American troops were proceeding successfully. However, ten days later, he ordered United States troops into neighboring Cambodia to clear out "enemy sanctuaries." (Unknown to Congress and the American people, U.S. planes already had been bombing Cambodia for over a year.) College students responded to Nixon's latest move with massive protests that exceeded anything yet seen. At Kent State University in Ohio, National Guardsmen called out during campus demonstrations fired into a crowd of students, killing four and wounding nine. Although Nixon deplored the incident, he reminded Americans "that when dissent turns to violence, it invites tragedy."

President Nixon's announcement of the American invasion of Cambodia was taken against the advice of most of his advisors. It would actually cause more problems both in Indochina and at home.

Ten days ago, in my report to the Nation on Vietnam, I announced a decision to withdraw an additional 150,000 Americans from Vietnam over the next year. I said then that I was making that decision despite our concern over increased enemy activity in Laos, in Cambodia, and in South Vietnam.

At that time, I warned that if I concluded that increased enemy activity in any of those areas endangered the lives of Americans remaining in Vietnam, I would not hesitate to take strong and effective measures to deal with that situation.

Despite that warning, North Vietnam has increased its military aggression in all these areas, and particularly in Cambodia.

After full consultation with the National Security Council, Ambassador Bunker, General Abrams, and my other advisers, I have concluded that the actions of the enemy in the last ten days clearly endanger the lives of Americans who are in Vietnam now and would constitute an unacceptable risk to those who will be there after withdrawal of another 150,000.

To protect our men who are in Vietnam and to guarantee the continued success of our withdrawal and Vietnamization programs, I have concluded that the time has come for action.

Tonight, I shall describe the actions of the enemy, the actions that I have ordered to deal with that situation, and the reasons for my decision.

Cambodia, a small country of seven million people, has been a neutral nation since the Geneva agreement of 1954—an agreement, incidentally, which was signed by the Government of North Vietnam. [. . .]

North Vietnam, however, has not respected that neutrality.

For the past five years—as indicated on this map that you see here—North Vietnam has occupied military sanctuaries all along the Cambodian frontier with South Vietnam. Some of these extend up to 20 miles into Cambodia. The sanctuaries are in red and, as you note, they are on both sides of the border. They are used for hit and run attacks on American and South Vietnamese forces in South Vietnam.

These Communist occupied territories contain major base camps, training sites, logistics facilities, weapons and ammunition factories, airstrips, and prisoner-of-war compounds.

For five years, neither the United States nor South Vietnam has moved against these enemy sanctuaries because we did not wish to violate the territory of a neutral nation. Even after the Vietnamese Communists began to expand these sanctuaries four weeks ago, we counseled patience to our South Vietnamese allies and imposed restraints on our own commanders.

In contrast to our policy, the enemy in the past two weeks has stepped up his guerrilla actions and he is concentrating his main forces in these sanctuaries that you see on this map where they are building up to launch massive attacks on our forces and those of South Vietnam.

North Vietnam in the last two weeks has stripped away all pretense of respecting the sovereignty or the neutrality of Cambodia. Thousands of their soldiers are invading the country from the sanctuaries; they are encircling the Phnom Penh. Coming from these sanctuaries, as you see here, they have moved to Cambodia and are encircling the capital.

Cambodia, as a result of this, has sent out a call to the United States, to a number of other nations, for assistance. Because if this enemy effort succeeds, Cambodia would become a vast enemy staging area and a springboard for attacks on South Vietnam along 600 miles of frontier—a refuge where enemy troops could return from combat without fear of retaliation.

North Vietnamese men and supplies could then be poured into that country, jeopardizing not only the lives of our own men but the people of South Vietnam as well.

Now confronted with this situation, we have three options. First, we can do nothing. Well, the ultimate result of that course of action is clear. Unless we

As President, Nixon prided himself on mastering grand strategies in foreign policy. However, a settlement of the Vietnam War, although his priority upon taking office, remained elusive. He wanted to negotiate an agreement that would bring American troops home but he wanted only "peace with honor," which meant preserving a pro-American South Vietnamese government. This strategy, called "Vietnamization," involved a gradual withdrawal of American troops, peace talks, and shifting the fighting to the South Vietnamese army. But it just did not work. The North Vietnamese continually insisted on complete American withdrawal and the abandonment of the South Vietnamese military government.

indulge in wishful thinking, the lives of Americans remaining in Vietnam after our next withdrawal of 150,000 would be gravely threatened. [. . .]

Our second choice is to provide massive military assistance to Cambodia itself. Now unfortunately, while we deeply sympathize with the plight of seven million Cambodians whose country is being invaded, massive amounts of military assistance could not be rapidly and effectively utilized by the small Cambodian Army against the immediate threat. With other nations, we shall do our best to provide the small arms and other equipment which the Cambodian Army of 40,000 needs and can use for its defense. But the aid we will provide will be limited to the purpose of enabling Cambodia to defend its neutrality and not for the purpose of making it an active belligerent on one side or the other.

Our third choice is to go to the heart of the trouble. That means cleaning out major North Vietnamese and Vietcong occupied territories—these sanctuaries which serve as bases for attacks on both Cambodia and American and South Vietnamese forces in South Vietnam. Some of these, incidentally, are as close to Saigon as Baltimore is to Washington. This one, for example, is called the Parrot's Beak. It is only 33 miles from Saigon.

Now faced with these three options, this is the decision I have made.

In cooperation with the armed forces of South Vietnam, attacks are being launched this week to clean out major enemy sanctuaries on the Cambodian-Vietnam border.

A major responsibility for the ground operations is being assumed by South Vietnamese forces. For example, the attacks in several areas, including the Parrot's Beak that I referred to a moment ago, are exclusively South Vietnamese ground operations under South Vietnamese command with the United States providing air and logistical support.

There is one area, however, immediately above Parrot's Beak, where I have concluded that a combined American and South Vietnamese operation is necessary.

Tonight, American and South Vietnamese units will attack the headquarters for the entire Communist military operation in South Vietnam. This key control center has been occupied by the North Vietnamese and Vietcong for five years in blatant violation of Cambodia's neutrality.

This is not an invasion of Cambodia. The areas in which these attacks will be launched are completely occupied and controlled by North Vietnamese forces. Our purpose is not to occupy the areas. Once enemy forces are driven out of these sanctuaries and once their military supplies are destroyed, we will withdraw.

These actions are in no way directed to the security interests of any nation. Any government that chooses to use these actions as a pretext for harming relations with the United States will be doing so on its own responsibility, and on its own initiative, and we will draw the appropriate conclusions.

Now let me give you the reasons for my decision.

A majority of the American people, a majority of you listening to me, are for the withdrawal of our forces from Vietnam. The action I have taken tonight is indispensable for the continuing success of that withdrawal program.

A majority of American people want to end this war rather than to have it drag on interminably. The action I have taken tonight will serve that purpose.

A majority of the American people want to keep the casualties of our brave men in Vietnam at an absolute minimum. The action I take tonight is essential if we are to accomplish that goal.

We take this action not for the purpose of expanding the war into Cambodia but for the purpose of ending the war in Vietnam and winning the just peace we all desire. We have made—we will continue to make every possible effort to end this war through negotiation at the conference table rather than through more fighting on the battlefield. [. . .]

Tonight, I again warn the North Vietnamese that if they continue to escalate the fighting when the United States is withdrawing its forces, I shall meet my responsibility as Commander in Chief of our Armed Forces to take the action I consider necessary to defend the security of our American men.

The action that I have announced tonight puts the leaders of North Vietnam on notice that we will be patient in working for peace; we will be conciliatory at the conference table, but we will not be humiliated. We will not be defeated. We will not allow American men by the thousands to be killed by an enemy from privileged sanctuaries.

The time came long ago to end this war through peaceful negotiations. We stand ready for those negotiations. We have made major efforts, many of which must remain secret. I say tonight: All. the offers and approaches made previously remain on the conference table whenever Hanoi is ready to negotiate seriously.

But if the enemy response to our most conciliatory offers for peaceful negotiation continues to be to increase its attacks and humiliate and defeat us, we shall react accordingly.

My fellow Americans, we live in an age of anarchy, both abroad and at home. We see mindless attacks on all the great institutions which have been created by free civilizations in the last 500 years. Even here in the United States, great universities are being systematically destroyed. Small nations all over the world find themselves under attack from within and from without.

If, when the chips are down, the world's most powerful nation, the United States of America, acts like a pitiful, helpless giant, the forces of totalitarianism and anarchy will threaten free nations and free institutions throughout the world.

It is not our power but our will and character that is being tested tonight. The question all Americans must ask and answer tonight is this: Does the richest and strongest nation in the history of the world have the character to meet a direct challenge by a group which rejects every effort to win a just peace, ignores our warning, tramples on solemn agreements, violates the neutrality of an unarmed people, and uses our prisoners as hostages?

If we fail to meet this challenge, all other nations will be on notice that despite its overwhelming power the United States, when a real crisis comes, will be found wanting.

During my campaign for the Presidency, I pledged to bring Americans home from Vietnam. They are coming home.

I promised to end that war. I shall keep that promise.

I promised to win a just peace. I shall keep that promise.

We shall avoid a wider war. But we are also determined to put an end to this war. [. . .]

No one is more aware than I am of the political consequences of the action I have taken. It is tempting to take the easy political path: to blame this war on previous administrations and to bring all of our men home immediately, regardless of the consequences, even though that would mean defeat for the United States; to desert 18 million South Vietnamese people, who have put their trust in us and to expose them to the same slaughter and savagery which the leaders of North Vietnam inflicted on hundreds of thousands of North Vietnamese who chose freedom when the Communists took over North Vietnam in 1954; to get peace at any price now, even though I know that a peace of humiliation for the United States would lead to a bigger war or surrender later.

I have rejected all political considerations in making this decision.

Whether my party gains in November is nothing compared to the lives of 400,000 brave Americans fighting for our country and for the cause of peace and freedom in Vietnam. Whether I may be a one-term President is insignificant compared to whether by our failure to act in this crisis the United States proves itself to be unworthy to lead the forces of freedom in this critical period in world history. I would rather be a one-term President and do what I believe is right than to be a two-term President at the cost of seeing America become a second-rate power and to see this Nation accept the first defeat in its proud 190-year history.

I realize that in this war there are honest and deep differences in this country about whether or not we should have become involved, that there are differences as to how the war should have been conducted. But the decision I announce tonight transcends those differences.

For the lives of American men are involved. The opportunity for 150,000 Americans to come home in the next 12 months is involved. The future of 18 million people in South Vietnam and seven million people in Cambodia is involved. The possibility of winning a just peace in Vietnam and in the Pacific is at stake.

It is customary to conclude a speech from the White House by asking support for the President of the United States. Tonight, I depart from that precedent. What I ask is far more important. I ask for your support for our brave men fighting tonight halfway around the world—not for territory—not for glory—but so that their younger brothers and their sons and your sons can have a chance to grow up in a world of peace and freedom and justice.

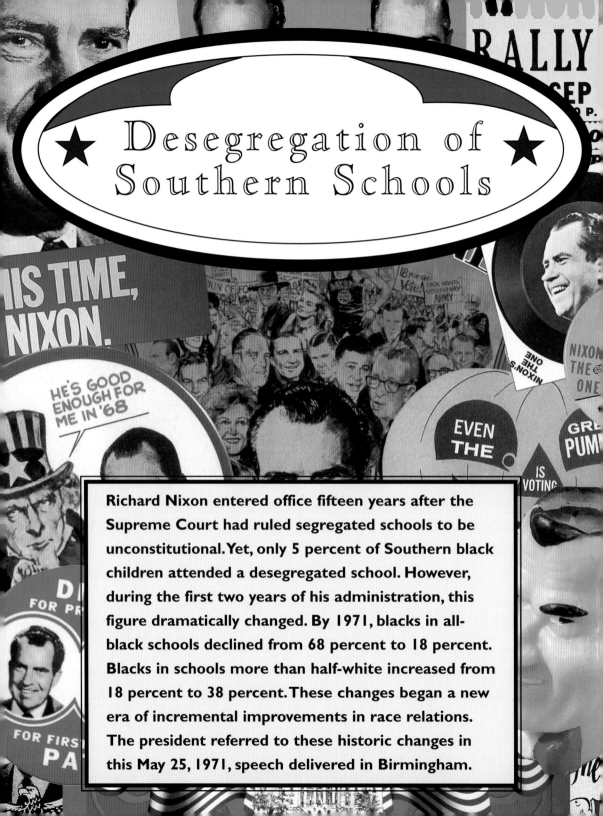

Desegregation of Southern Schools

Richard Nixon entered office fifteen years after the Supreme Court had ruled segregated schools to be unconstitutional. Yet, only 5 percent of Southern black children attended a desegregated school. However, during the first two years of his administration, this figure dramatically changed. By 1971, blacks in all-black schools declined from 68 percent to 18 percent. Blacks in schools more than half-white increased from 18 percent to 38 percent. These changes began a new era of incremental improvements in race relations. The president referred to these historic changes in this May 25, 1971, speech delivered in Birmingham.

[. . .] I spoke in Mobile of the fact that we have differences between regions, we have differences between races, we have differences between religions, we have differences between the generations today, and these differences have at times been very destructive. We must recognize that we will always have those differences. People of different races, different religions, from different backgrounds, and of different ages are not always going to agree.

The question is, can those differences be resolved peacefully, and second, can they be made creative rather than destructive? Must they be a drain upon us? Must they go so far that they destroy the confidence and faith of this great Nation in its destiny and its future? I do not believe that that is necessary.

Two specific points that I would like to mention. I would say this in the North if I were speaking there; I say it in the South. I know the difficult problems most of you in the Southern States have had on the school desegregation problem. I went to school in the South, and so, therefore, I am more familiar with how Southerners feel about that problem than others. Also, I went to school in the North, or the West I should say, and I have nothing but utter contempt for the double hypocritical standard of Northerners who look at the South and point the finger and say, "Why don't those Southerners do something about their race problem?"

Let's look at the facts. In the past year, two years, there has been a peaceful, relatively quiet, very significant revolution. Oh, it is not over, there are problems—there was one in Chattanooga, I understand, the last couple days; there will be more. But look what has happened in the South. Today 38 percent of all black children in the South go to majority white schools. Today only 28 percent of all black children in the North go to majority white schools. There has been no progress in the North in the

Celluloid button for Nixon, casting him in the tradition of Lincoln, Washington, and Roosevelt.

past two years in that respect. There has been significant progress in the South.

How did it come about? It came about because farsighted leaders in the South, black and white, some of whom I am sure did not agree with the opinions handed down by the Supreme Court which were the law of the land, recognized as law-abiding citizens that they had the responsibility to meet that law of the land, and they had dealt with the problem—not completely, there is more yet to be done. The recent decision of the Supreme Court presents some more problems, but I am confident that over a period of time those problems will also be handled in a peaceful and orderly way for the most part.

But let's look at the deeper significance of this. As I speak today in what is called the Heart of Dixie, I realize that America at this time needs to become one country. Too long we have been divided. It has been North versus South versus West; Wall Street versus the country and the country versus the city and the rest. That doesn't mean we don't have differences and will not continue to have them, but those regional differences, it seems to me, must go. Presidents of the United States should come to Alabama and Mississippi and Georgia and Louisiana more than once, more often than every 50 years or every 100 years as the case might be, to some of the cities, and they should come because this is one nation, and we must speak as one nation, we must work as one nation. [. . .]

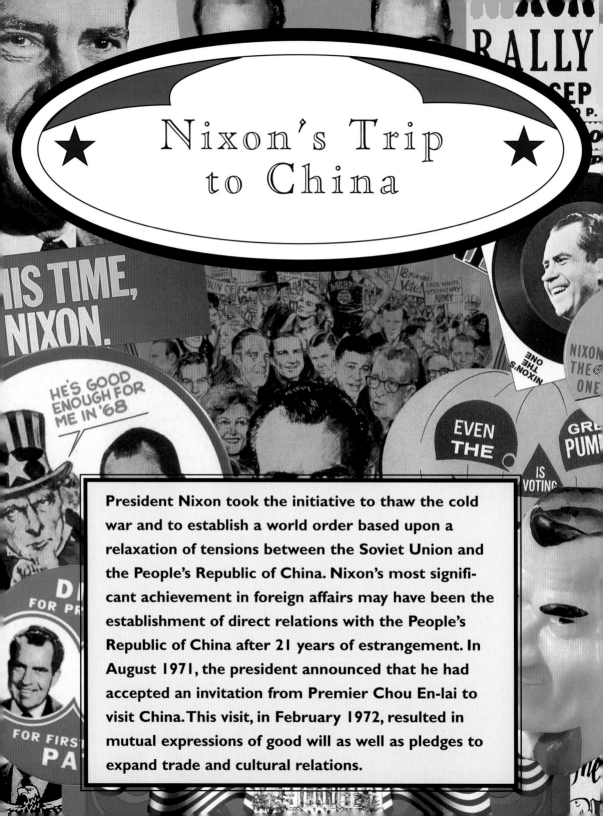

Nixon's Trip to China

President Nixon took the initiative to thaw the cold war and to establish a world order based upon a relaxation of tensions between the Soviet Union and the People's Republic of China. Nixon's most significant achievement in foreign affairs may have been the establishment of direct relations with the People's Republic of China after 21 years of estrangement. In August 1971, the president announced that he had accepted an invitation from Premier Chou En-lai to visit China. This visit, in February 1972, resulted in mutual expressions of good will as well as pledges to expand trade and cultural relations.

I have requested this television time tonight to announce a major development in our efforts to build a lasting peace in the world.

As I have pointed out on a number of occasions over the past three years, there can be no stable and enduring peace without the participation of the People's Republic of China and its 750 million people. That is why I have undertaken initiatives in several areas to open the door for more normal relations between our two countries.

In pursuance of that goal, I sent Dr. Kissinger, my Assistant for National Security Affairs, to Peking during his recent world tour for the purpose of having talks with Premier Chou En-lai. The announcement I shall now read is being issued simultaneously in Peking and in the United States.

Premier Chou En-lai and Dr. Henry Kissinger, President Nixon's Assistant for National Security Affairs, held talks in Peking from July 9 to 11, 1971. Knowing of President Nixon's expressed desire to visit the People's Republic of China, Premier Chou En-lai, on behalf of the Government of the People's Republic of China, has extended an invitation to President Nixon to visit China at an appropriate date before May 1972. President Nixon has accepted the invitation with pleasure.

The meeting between the leaders of China and the United States is to seek the normalization of relations between the two countries and also to exchange views on questions of concern to the two sides. In anticipation of the inevitable speculation which will follow this announcement, I want to put our policy in the clearest possible context. [. . .]

I have taken this action because of my profound conviction that all nations will gain from a reduction of tensions and a better relationship between the United States and the People's Republic of China.

It is in that spirit that I will undertake what I deeply hope will become a journey for peace, peace not just for our generation, but for future generations on this earth we share together.

Second Inaugural Address

In August 1972, Richard Nixon and Vice President Spiro Agnew were renominated at the Republican Convention in Miami Beach. They had an insurmountable lead. Nixon became the favorite not only of Republicans but of many Democrats and Independents. He carried every state except Massachusetts and the District of Columbia, receiving 520 electoral votes to George McGovern's 17. Nixon received 60.7 percent of the popular vote which was second only to Lyndon Johnson's record-breaking 61.1 percent in the landslide of 1964. Nixon swept the Solid South, completely capturing the George Wallace vote. However, Nixon noted in his diary that he was overcome by "a curious feeling, perhaps a foreboding, that muted my enjoyment of this triumphal moment."

On January 20, 1973, Nixon was inaugurated for his second term. In his *Memoirs*, there is no mention of the event. He had hoped to be able to announce that peace had been achieved in Vietnam but this was not possible. The hoopla which ordinarily occurs at inaugurals was distinctly absent. Nixon's inaugural address was short and somber.

When we met here four years ago, America was bleak in spirit, depressed by the prospect of seemingly endless war abroad and of destructive conflict at home.

As we meet here today, we stand on the threshold of a new era of peace in the world.

The central question before us is: How shall we use that peace? Let us resolve that this era we are about to enter will not be what other postwar periods have so often been: a time of retreat and isolation that leads to stagnation at home and invites new danger abroad.

Let us resolve that this will be what it can become: a time of great responsibilities greatly borne, in which we renew the spirit and the promise of America as we enter our third century as a nation.

This past year saw far-reaching results from our new policies for peace. By continuing to revitalize our traditional friendships, and by our missions to Peking and to Moscow, we were able to establish the base for a new and more durable pattern of relationships among the nations of the world. Because of America's bold initiatives, 1972 will be long remembered as the year of the greatest progress since the end of World War II toward a lasting peace in the world.

The peace we seek in the world is not the flimsy peace which is merely an interlude between wars, but a peace which can endure for generations to come.

It is important that we understand both the necessity and the limitations of America's role in maintaining that peace. Unless we in America work to preserve the peace, there will be no peace. Unless we in America work to preserve freedom, there will be no freedom.

But let us clearly understand the new nature of America's role, as a result of the new policies we have adopted over these past four years.

We shall respect our treaty commitments.

We shall support vigorously the principle that no country has the right to impose its will or rule on another by force.

We shall continue, in this era of negotiation, to work for the limitation of nuclear arms, and to reduce the danger of confrontation between the great powers.

We shall do our share in defending peace and freedom in the world. But we shall expect others to do their share.

The time has passed when America will make every other nation's conflict our own, or make every other nation's future our responsibility, or presume to tell the people of other nations how to manage their own affairs.

Just as we respect the right of each nation to determine its own future, we also recognize the responsibility of each nation to secure its own future.

Just as America's role is indispensable in preserving the world's peace, so is each nation's role indispensable in preserving its own peace.

Together with the rest of the world, let us resolve to move forward from the beginnings we have made. Let us continue to bring down the walls of hostility which have divided the world for too long, and to build in their place bridges of understanding—so that despite profound differences between systems of government, the people of the world can be friends.

Let us build a structure of peace in the world in which the weak are as safe as the strong—in which each respects the right of the other to live by a different system—in which those who would influence others will do so by the strength of their ideas, and not by the force of their arms.

Let us accept that high responsibility not as a burden, but gladly—gladly because the chance to build such a peace is the noblest endeavor in which a nation can engage; gladly, also, because only if we act greatly in meeting our responsibilities abroad will we remain a great Nation, and only if we remain a great Nation will we act greatly in meeting our challenges at home.

We have the chance today to do more than ever before in our history to make life better in America—to ensure better education, better health, better housing, better transportation, a cleaner environment—to restore respect for law, to make our communities more livable—and to insure the God-given right of every American to full and equal opportunity.

Because the range of our needs is so great—because the reach of our opportunities is so great—let us be bold in our determination to meet those needs in new ways.

Just as building a structure of peace abroad has required turning away from old policies that failed, so building a new era of progress at home requires turning away from old policies that have failed.

Abroad, the shift from old policies to new has not been a retreat from our responsibilities, but a better way to peace.

And at home, the shift from old policies to new will not be a retreat from our responsibilities, but a better way to progress.

Abroad and at home, the key to those new responsibilities lies in the placing and the division of responsibility. We have lived too long with the consequences of attempting to gather all power and responsibility in Washington.

Abroad and at home, the time has come to turn away from the condescending policies of paternalism—of "Washington knows best."

A person can be expected to act responsibly only if he has responsibility. This is human nature. So let us encourage individuals at home and nations abroad to do more for themselves, to decide more for themselves. Let us locate responsibility in more places. Let us measure what we will do for others by what they will do for themselves.

That is why today I offer no promise of a purely governmental solution for every problem. We have lived too long with that false promise. In trusting too much in government, we have asked of it more than it can deliver. This leads only to inflated expectations, to reduced individual effort, and to a disappointment and frustration that erode confidence both in what government can do and in what people can do. Government must learn to take less from people so that people can do more for themselves.

Let us remember that America was built not by government, but by people—not by welfare, but by work—not by shirking responsibility, but by seeking responsibility.

In our own lives, let each of us ask—not just what will government do for me, but what can I do for myself?

In the challenges we face together, let each of us ask—not just how can government help, but how can I help?

Your National Government has a great and vital role to play. And I pledge to you that where this Government should act, we will act boldly and we will lead boldly. But just as important is the role that each and every one of us must play, as an individual and as a member of his own community.

From this day forward, let each of us make a solemn commitment in his own heart: to bear his responsibility, to do his part, to live his ideals—so that together, we can see the dawn of a new age of progress for America, and together, as we celebrate our 200th anniversary as a nation, we can do so proud in the fulfillment of our promise to ourselves and to the world.

As America's longest and most difficult war comes to an end, let us again learn to debate our differences with civility and decency. And let each of us reach out for that one precious quality government cannot provide—a new level of respect for the rights and feelings of one another, a new level of respect for the individual human dignity which is the cherished birthright of every American.

Above all else, the time has come for us to renew our faith in ourselves and in America.

In recent years, that faith has been challenged. Our children have been taught to be ashamed of their country, ashamed of their parents, ashamed of America's record at home and of its role in the world. At every turn, we have been beset by those who find everything wrong with America and little that is right. But I am confident that this will not be the judgment of history on these remarkable times in which we are privileged to live.

America's record in this century has been unparalleled in the world's history for its responsibility, for its generosity, for its creativity, and for its progress.

Let us be proud that our system has produced and provided more freedom and more abundance, more widely shared, than any other system in the history of the world.

Let us be proud that in each of the four wars in which we have been engaged in this century, including the one we are now bringing to an end, we have fought not for our selfish advantage, but to help others resist aggression.

Let us be proud that by our bold, new initiatives, and by our steadfastness for peace with honor, we have made a breakthrough toward creating in the world what the world has not known before—a structure of peace that can last, not merely for our time, but for generations to come.

We are embarking here today on an era that presents challenges great as those any nation, or any generation, has ever faced.

We shall answer to God, to history, and to our conscience for the way in which we use these years.

As I stand in this place, so hallowed by history, I think of others who have stood here before me. I think of the dreams they had for America, and I think of how each recognized that he needed help far beyond himself in order to make those dreams come true.

Today, I ask your prayers that in the years ahead I may have God's help in making decisions that are right for America, and I pray for your help so that together we may be worthy of our challenge.

Let us pledge together to make these next four years the best four years in America's history, so that on its 200th birthday America will be as young and as vital as when it began, and as bright a beacon of hope for all the world.

Let us go forward from here confident in hope, strong in our faith in one another, sustained by our faith in God who created us, and striving always to serve His purpose.

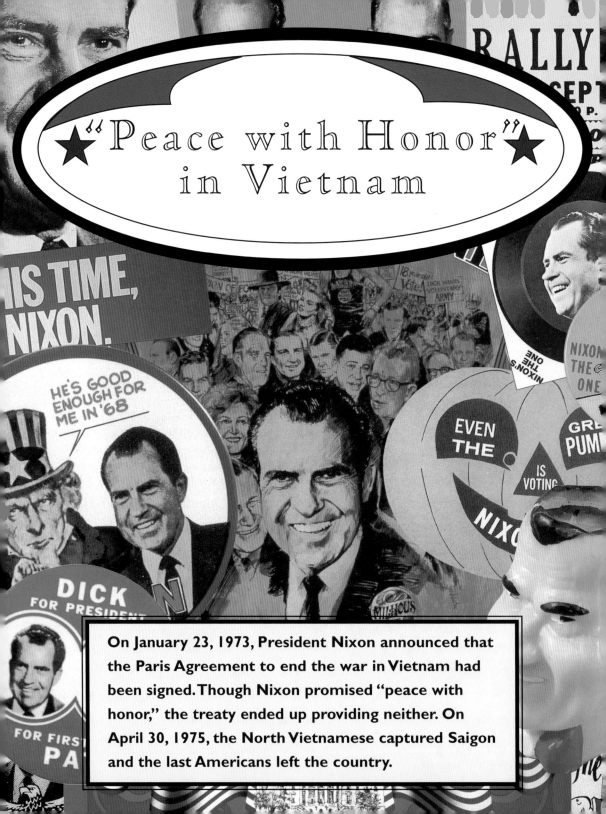

"Peace with Honor" in Vietnam

RALLY
SEPT
O P.

IS TIME,
NIXON.

HE'S GOOD ENOUGH FOR ME IN '68

NIXON'S
THE ONE

NIXON
THE
ONE

EVEN
THE

GRE
PUM

IS
VOTING

NIX

DICK
FOR PRESIDENT

FOR FIRS
PA

On January 23, 1973, President Nixon announced that the Paris Agreement to end the war in Vietnam had been signed. Though Nixon promised "peace with honor," the treaty ended up providing neither. On April 30, 1975, the North Vietnamese captured Saigon and the last Americans left the country.

Good evening. I have asked for this radio and television time tonight for the purpose of announcing that we today have concluded an agreement to end the war and bring peace with honor in Vietnam and in Southeast Asia.

The following statement is being issued at this moment in Washington and Hanoi:

> At 12:30 Paris time today [Tuesday], January 23, 1973, the Agreement on Ending the War and Restoring Peace in Vietnam was initialed by Dr. Henry Kissinger on behalf of the United States, and Special Adviser Le Duc Tho on behalf of the Democratic Republic of Vietnam.
>
> The agreement will be formally signed by the parties participating in the Paris Conference on Vietnam on January 27, 1973, at the International Conference Center in Paris.
>
> The cease-fire will take effect at 2400 Greenwich Mean Time, January 27, 1973. The United States and the Democratic Republic of Vietnam express the hope that this agreement will insure stable peace in Vietnam and contribute to the preservation of lasting peace in Indochina and Southeast Asia.

That concludes the formal statement.

Throughout the years of negotiations, we have insisted on peace with honor. In my addresses to the Nation from this room of January 25 and May 8, [1972] I set forth the goals that we considered essential for peace with honor.

In the settlement that has now been agreed to, all the conditions that I laid down then have been met. A cease-fire, internationally supervised, will begin at 7 P.M., this Saturday, January 27, Washington time. Within 60 days from this Saturday, all Americans held prisoners of war throughout Indochina will be released. There will be the fullest possible accounting for all of those who are missing in action.

During the same 60-day period, all American forces will be withdrawn from South Vietnam.

The people of South Vietnam have been guaranteed the right to determine their own future, without outside interference.

By joint agreement, the full text of the agreement and the protocols to carry it out, will be issued tomorrow.

Throughout these negotiations we have been in the closest consultation with President Thieu and other representatives of the Republic of Vietnam. This settlement meets the goals and has the full support of President Thieu and the Government of the Republic of Vietnam, as well as that of our other allies who are affected.

The United States will continue to recognize the Government of the Republic of Vietnam as the sole legitimate government of South Vietnam.

We shall continue to aid South Vietnam within the terms of the agreement and we shall support efforts by the people of South Vietnam to settle their problems peacefully among themselves.

We must recognize that ending the war is only the first step toward building the peace. All parties must now see to it that this is a peace that lasts, and also a peace that heals, and a peace that not only ends the war in Southeast Asia, but contributes to the prospects of peace in the whole world.

This will mean that the terms of the agreement must be scrupulously adhered to. We shall do everything the agreement requires of us and we shall expect the other parties to do everything it requires of them. We shall also expect other interested nations to help insure that the agreement is carried out and peace is maintained.

As this long and very difficult war ends, I would like to address a few special words to each of those who have been parties in the conflict.

First, to the people and Government of South Vietnam: By your courage, by your sacrifice, you have won the precious right to determine your own future and you have developed the strength to defend that right. We look

1972 campaign cigarette packets for Nixon and McGovern.

Throughout 1972, Nixon was obsessed with winning the presidential election. In 1968, he had won in a three-way race, receiving a plurality of the popular vote. Now, in an anticipated two-candidate race, Nixon had to dramatically increase his popular vote. With the aid of his chief political advisor Attorney General John Mitchell, Nixon devised a reelection plan which was aimed at the "real majority" in the United States—the "unyoung, unblack, and unpoor": the mature, white, middle-class citizen who was disgusted with campus protests, school integration, street crime, and rising health care costs.

Nixon was far more interested in his Democratic opponent than in any particular campaign issue. The opponents Nixon most feared were Senator Edmund Muskie of Maine and Governor George Wallace of Alabama. He hoped that the Democrats would nominate George McGovern, the liberal senator from South Dakota. Nixon later wrote: "If by some miracle [McGovern] would be nominated, I had no doubt that he would be the easiest Democrat to beat."

forward to working with you in the future, friends in peace as we have been allies in war.

To the leaders of North Vietnam: As we have ended the war through negotiations, let us now build a peace of reconciliation. For our part, we are prepared to make a major effort to help achieve that goal. But just as reciprocity was needed to end the war, so, too, will it be needed to build and strengthen the peace.

To the other major powers that have been involved even indirectly: Now is the time for mutual restraint so that the peace we have achieved can last.

And finally, to all of you who are listening, the American people: Your steadfastness in supporting our insistence on peace with honor has made peace with honor possible. I know that you would not have wanted that peace jeopardized. With our secret negotiations at the sensitive stage they were in during this recent period, for me to have discussed publicly our efforts to secure peace would not only have violated our understanding with North Vietnam, it would have seriously harmed and possibly destroyed the chances for peace. Therefore, I know that you now can understand why, during these past several weeks, I have not made any public statements about those efforts.

The important thing was not to talk about peace, but to get peace and to get the right kind of peace. This we have done.

Now that we have achieved an honorable agreement, let us be proud that America did not settle for a peace that would have betrayed our allies, that would have abandoned our prisoners of war, or that would have ended the war for us but would have continued the war for the 50 million people of Indochina. Let us be proud of the 2.5 million young Americans who served in Vietnam, who served with honor and distinction in one of the most selfless enterprises in the history of nations. And let us be proud of those who sacrificed, who gave their lives so that the people of South Vietnam might live in freedom and so that the world might live in peace.

In particular, I would like to say a word to some of the bravest people I have ever met—the wives, the children, the families of our prisoners of war and the missing in action. When others called on us to settle on any terms, you had the courage to stand for the right kind of peace so that those who died and those who suffered would not have died and suffered in vain, and so that, where this generation knew war, the next generation would know peace. Nothing means more to me at this moment than the fact that your long vigil is coming to an end.

Just yesterday, a great American, who once occupied this office, died. In his life President Johnson endured the vilification of those who sought to portray him as a man of war. But there was nothing he cared about more deeply than achieving a lasting peace in the world.

I remember the last time I talked with him. It was just the day after New Year's. He spoke then of his concern with bringing peace, with making it the right kind of peace, and I was grateful that he once again expressed his support for my efforts to gain such a peace. No one would have welcomed this peace more than he.

And I know he would join me in asking for those who died and for those who live, let us consecrate this moment by resolving together to make the peace we have achieved a peace that will last.

Thank you and good evening.

Articles of
Impeachment

The constitutional procedure for removing a president from office is called impeachment. Article II, Section 4 of the Constitution provides that the president "shall be removed from office on Impeachment for, and conviction of, Treason, Bribery, or other high Crimes and Misdemeanors." The House of Representatives initiates the procedure by voting an accusation—an impeachment. Only three presidents have been the subject of impeachment proceedings—Andrew Johnson (1868); Richard Nixon (1974) and Bill Clinton (1998).

On July 27, 1974, the House Judiciary Committee, after a lengthy investigation, recommended the impeachment of President Nixon by the House of Representatives. They charged the president with impeding the course of justice, violating individual rights by using federal agencies for illegal purposes, and failing to produce evidence the committee had requested. The seriousness of each charge is detailed in the following three impeachment charges voted by the committee.

Resolved, that Richard M. Nixon, President of the United States, is impeached for high crimes and misdemeanors, and that the following articles of impeachment are to be exhibited to the Senate:

Article 1

In his conduct of the office of President of the United States, Richard M. Nixon, in violation of his constitutional oath faithfully to execute the office of President of the United States and, to the best of his ability, preserve, protect, and defend the Constitution of the United States, and in violation of his constitutional duty to take care that the laws be faithfully executed, has prevented, obstructed, and impeded the administration of justice, in that:

On June 17, 1972, and prior thereto, agents of the Committee for the Re-election of the President committed unlawful entry of the headquarters of the Democratic National Committee in Washington, District of Columbia, for the purpose of securing political intelligence. Subsequent thereto, Richard M. Nixon, using the powers of his high office, engaged personally and through his close subordinates and agents, in a course of conduct or plan designed to delay, impede, and obstruct the investigation of such illegal entry; to cover up, conceal and protect those responsible; and to conceal the existence and scope of other unlawful covert activities.

The means used to implement this course of conduct or plan included one or more of the following:

1. Making false or misleading statements to lawfully authorized investigative officers and employees of the United States;

2. Withholding relevant and material evidence or information from lawfully authorized investigative officers and employees of the United States;

3. Approving, condoning, acquiescing in, and counseling witnesses

with respect to the giving of false or misleading statements to lawfully authorized investigative officers and employees of the United States and false or misleading testimony in duly instituted judicial and congressional proceedings;

4. Interfering or endeavoring to interfere with the conduct of investigations by the Department of Justice of the United States, the Federal Bureau of Investigation, the office of Watergate Special Prosecution Force, and Congressional Committees;

5. Approving, condoning, and acquiescing in, the surreptitious payment of substantial sums of money for the purpose of obtaining the silence or influencing the testimony of witnesses, potential witnesses or individuals who participated in such unlawful entry and other illegal activities;

6. Endeavoring to misuse the Central Intelligence Agency, an agency of the United States;

7. Disseminating information received from officers of the Department of Justice of the United States to subjects of investigations conducted by lawfully authorized investigative officers and employees of the United States, for the purpose of aiding and assisting such subjects in their attempts to avoid criminal liability;

8. Making or causing to be made false or misleading public statements for the purpose of deceiving the people of the United States into believing that a thorough and complete investigation had been conducted with respect to allegations of misconduct on the part of personnel of the executive branch of the United States and personnel of the Committee for the Re-election of the President, and that there was no involvement of such personnel in such misconduct; or

9. Endeavoring to cause prospective defendants, and individuals duly tried and convicted, to expect favored treatment and consideration in return for their silence or false testimony, or rewarding individuals for their silence or false testimony.

In all of this, Richard M. Nixon has acted in a manner contrary to his trust as President and subversive of constitutional government, to the great prejudice of the cause of law and justice and to the manifest injury of the people of the United States.

Wherefore Richard M. Nixon, by such conduct, warrants impeachment and trial, and removal from office.

Article 2

Using the powers of the office of President of the United States, Richard M. Nixon, in violation of his constitutional oath faithfully to execute the office of President of the United States and, to the best of his ability, preserve, protect, and defend the Constitution of the United States, and in disregard of his constitutional duty to take care that the laws be faithfully executed, has repeatedly engaged in conduct violating the constitutional rights of citizens, impairing the due and proper administration of justice and the conduct of lawful inquiries, or contravening the laws governing agencies of the executive branch and the purposed of these agencies.

This conduct has included one or more of the following:

1. He has, acting personally and through his subordinates and agents, endeavored to obtain from the Internal Revenue Service, in violation of the constitutional rights of citizens, confidential information contained in income tax returns for purposed not authorized by law, and to cause, in violation of the constitutional rights of citizens, income tax audits or other income tax investigations to be initiated or conducted in a discriminatory manner.

2. He misused the Federal Bureau of Investigation, the Secret Service, and other executive personnel, in violation or disregard of the constitutional rights of citizens, by directing or authorizing such agencies or personnel to conduct or continue electronic surveillance or other investigations for purposes unrelated to national security, the enforcement of laws, or any other lawful function of his office; he did direct, authorize, or permit the use of information

obtained thereby for purposes unrelated to national security, the enforcement of laws, or any other lawful function of his office; and he did direct the concealment of certain records made by the Federal Bureau of Investigation of electronic surveillance.

3. He has, acting personally and through his subordinates and agents, in violation or disregard of the constitutional rights of citizens, authorized and permitted to be maintained a secret investigative unit within the office of the President, financed in part with money derived from campaign contributions, which unlawfully utilized the resources of the Central Intelligence Agency, engaged in covert and unlawful activities, and attempted to prejudice the constitutional right of an accused to a fair trial.

4. He has failed to take care that the laws were faithfully executed by failing to act when he knew or had reason to know that his close subordinates endeavored to impede and frustrate lawful inquiries by duly constituted executive, judicial and legislative entities concerning the unlawful entry into the headquarters of the Democratic National Committee, and the cover-up thereof, and concerning other unlawful activities including those relating to the confirmation of Richard Kleindienst as Attorney General of the United States, the electronic surveillance of private citizens, the break-in into the offices of Dr. Lewis Fielding, and the campaign financing practices of the Committee to Re-elect the President.

5. In disregard of the rule of law, he knowingly misused the executive power by interfering with agencies of the executive branch, including the Federal Bureau of Investigation, the Criminal Division, and the Office of Watergate Special Prosecution Force, of the Department of Justice, and the Central Intelligence Agency, in violation of his duty to take care that the laws be faithfully executed.

In all of this, Richard M. Nixon has acted in a manner contrary to his trust as President and subversive of constitutional government, to the great prejudice of the cause of law and justice and to the manifest injury of the people of the United States.

Wherefore Richard M. Nixon, by such conduct, warrants impeachment and trial, and removal from office.

Article 3

In his conduct of the office of President of the United States, Richard M. Nixon, contrary to his oath faithfully to execute the office of President of the United States and, to the best of his ability, preserve, protect, and defend the Constitution of the United States, and in violation of his constitutional duty to take care that the laws be faithfully executed, has failed without lawful cause or excuse to produce papers and things as directed by duly authorized subpoenas issued by the Committee on the Judiciary of the House of Representatives on April 11, 1974, May 15, 1974, May 30, 1974, and June 24, 1974, and willfully disobeyed such subpoenas. The subpoenaed papers and things were deemed necessary by the Committee in order to resolve by direct evidence fundamental, factual questions relating to Presidential direction, knowledge or approval of actions demonstrated by other evidence to be substantial grounds for impeachment of the President. In refusing to produce these papers and things Richard M. Nixon, substituting his judgment as to what materials were necessary for the inquiry, interposed the powers of the Presidency against the the lawful subpoenas of the House of Representatives, thereby assuming to himself functions and judgments necessary to the exercise of the sole power of impeachment vested by the Constitution in the House of Representatives.

In all of this, Richard M. Nixon has acted in a manner contrary to his trust as President and subversive of constitutional government, to the great prejudice of the cause of law and justice, and to the manifest injury of the people of the United States.

Wherefore, Richard M. Nixon, by such conduct, warrants impeachment and trial, and removal from office.

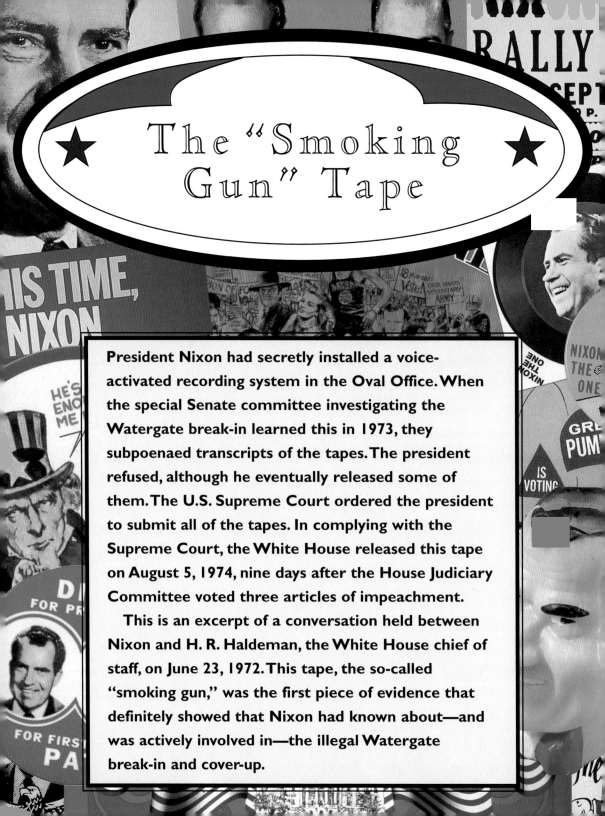

The "Smoking Gun" Tape

President Nixon had secretly installed a voice-activated recording system in the Oval Office. When the special Senate committee investigating the Watergate break-in learned this in 1973, they subpoenaed transcripts of the tapes. The president refused, although he eventually released some of them. The U.S. Supreme Court ordered the president to submit all of the tapes. In complying with the Supreme Court, the White House released this tape on August 5, 1974, nine days after the House Judiciary Committee voted three articles of impeachment.

This is an excerpt of a conversation held between Nixon and H. R. Haldeman, the White House chief of staff, on June 23, 1972. This tape, the so-called "smoking gun," was the first piece of evidence that definitely showed that Nixon had known about—and was actively involved in—the illegal Watergate break-in and cover-up.

Haldeman: Now, on the investigation, you know, the Democratic break-in thing, we're back to the—in the, the problem area because the FBI is not under control, because Gray* doesn't exactly know how to control them, and they have, their investigation is now leading into some productive areas, because they've been able to trace the money, not through the money itself, but through the bank, you know, sources—the banker himself. And, and it goes in some directions we don't want it to go. Ah, also there have been some things, like an informant came in off the street to the FBI in Miami, who was a photographer or has a friend who is a photographer who developed some films through this guy, Barker*, and the films had pictures of Democratic National Committee letterhead documents and things. So I guess, so it's things like that that are gonna, that are filtering in. Mitchell* came up with yesterday, and John Dean* analyzed very carefully last night and concludes, concurs now with Mitchell's recommendation that the only way to solve this, and we're set up beautifully to do it, ah, in that and that—the only network that paid any attention to it last night was NBC—they did a massive story on the Cuban thing.

Nixon: That's right.

Haldeman: That the way to handle this now is for us to have Walters* call Pat Gray and just say, "Stay the hell out of this . . . this is ah, business here we don't want you to go any further on it." That's not an unusual development, and ah, that would take care of it.

Nixon: What about Pat Gray—you mean Pat Gray doesn't want to?

Haldeman: Pat does want to. He doesn't know how to, and he doesn't have, he doesn't have any basis for doing it. Given this, he will then have the basis. He'll call Mark Felt* in, and the two of them—and Mark Felt

---

* Watergate figure whose role in the Nixon administration or the break-in and cover-up is explained in the sidebar on p. 116.

Watergate players mentioned during the June 23, 1972, Nixon-Haldeman meeting

L. Patrick Gray III: acting director of the Federal Bureau of Investigation (FBI) in 1972.

Bernard L. Barker: one of the five men caught in the Watergate break-in, June 17, 1972.

John N. Mitchell: attorney general from 1969 to 1972, when he resigned to serve as director of the Committee to Re-elect the President.

John Dean: White House counsel during the Nixon administration; he gave damning testimony during the Watergate hearings.

Vernon A. Walters: deputy director of the Central Intelligence Agency (CIA) in 1972.

W. Mark Felt: deputy associate director of the FBI in 1972.

Maurice H. Stans: finance chairman of the Committee to Re-elect the President

Richard C. Helms: director of the Central Intelligence Agency (CIA) in 1972.

John D. Ehrlichman: Nixon's domestic policy chief; he created a White House group called the "plumbers" intended to stop leaks to the media.

E. Howard Hunt Jr.: a former White House aide.

G. Gordon Liddy: former FBI agent associated with the Committee to Re-elect the President's campaign of "dirty tricks" during the 1972 election.

Charles W. Colson: White House special counsel.

wants to cooperate because he's ambitious . . .

Nixon: Yeah.

Haldeman: He'll call him in and say, "We've got the signal from across the river to, to put the hold on this." And that will fit rather well because the FBI agents who are working the case, at this point, feel that's what it is. This is CIA.

Nixon: But they've traced the money to 'em.

Haldeman: Well they have, they've traced to a name, but they haven't gotten to the guy yet.

Nixon: Would it be somebody here?

Haldeman: Ken Dahlberg.

Nixon: Who the hell is Ken Dahlberg?

Haldeman: He's ah, he gave $25,000 in Minnesota and ah, the check went directly in to this, to this guy Barker.

Nixon: He didn't get this from the committee though, from Stans*.

Haldeman: Yeah. It is. It is. It's directly traceable and there's some more through some Texas people in—that went to the Mexican bank which they can also trace to the Mexican bank . . . they'll get their names today. And (pause)

Nixon: Well, I mean, ah, there's no way. . . . I'm just thinking if they don't cooperate, what do they say? They they, they were approached by the Cubans. That's what Dahlberg has to say, the Texans too. Is that the idea?

Haldeman: Well, if they will. But then we're relying on more and more people all the time. That's the problem. And ah, they'll stop if we could, if we take this other step.

Nixon: All right. Fine.

Haldeman: And, and you seem to feel the thing to do is get them to stop?

Nixon: Right, fine.

Haldeman: They say the only way to do that is from White House instructions. And it's got to be to Helms* and, ah, what's his name . . . ? Walters.

Nixon: Walters.

Haldeman: And the proposal would be that Ehrlichman* [coughs] and I call them in and say, ah. . . .

Nixon: How do you call him in, I mean you just, well, we protected Helms from one hell of a lot of things.

Haldeman: That's what Ehrlichman says.

Nixon: Of course, this is a [hunt] that will uncover a lot of things. You open that scab there's a hell of a lot of things and that we just feel that it would be very detrimental to have this thing go any further. This involves these Cubans, Hunt*, and a lot of hanky-panky that we have nothing to do with ourselves. Well what the hell, did Mitchell know about this thing to any much of a degree?

Haldeman: I think so. I don't think he knew the details, but I think he knew.

Nixon: He didn't know how it was going to be handled though, with Dahlberg and the Texans and so forth? Well who was the [idiot] that did? [Unintelligible] Is it Liddy*? Is that the fellow? He must be a little nuts.

Haldeman: He is.

Nixon: I mean he just isn't well screwed on is he? Isn't that the problem?

Haldeman: No, but he was under pressure, apparently, to get more information, and as he got more pressure, he pushed the people harder to move harder on. . . .

Nixon: Pressure from Mitchell?

Haldeman: Apparently.

Nixon: Oh, Mitchell, Mitchell was at the point that you made on this, that exactly what I need from you is on the—

Haldeman: Gemstone, yeah.

Nixon: All right, fine, I understand it all. We won't second-guess Mitchell and the rest. Thank God it wasn't Colson*.

Haldeman: The FBI interviewed Colson yesterday. They determined that would be a good thing to do. To have him take an interrogation, which he did, and that, the FBI guys working the case had concluded that there were one or two possibilities, one, that this was a White House, they don't think that there is anything at the Election Committee, they think it was either a White House operation and they had some obscure reasons for it, non-political, or it was Cubans and the CIA. And after their interrogation of, of Colson, yesterday, they concluded it was not the White House, but are now convinced it is a CIA thing, so the CIA turn off would . . .

Nixon: Well, not sure of their analysis, I'm not going to get that involved. I'm [unintelligible].

Haldeman: No, sir. We don't want you to.

Nixon: You call them in. [pause] Good. Good deal! Play it tough. That's the way they play it and that's the way we are going to play it.

Haldeman: OK. We'll do it.

Nixon: Yeah, when I saw that news summary item, I of course knew it was a bunch of crap, but I thought ah, well it's good to have them off on this wild hair thing because when they start bugging us, which they have, we'll know our little boys will not know how to handle it. I hope they will though. You never know. Maybe, you think about it. Good!

[Other matters are discussed before the conversation returns to the strategy to cover up the Committee to Re-elect the President's role in the break-in.]

Nixon: When you get in these people when you . . . get these people in, say: "Look, the problem is that this will open the whole, the whole Bay of Pigs thing, and the President just feels that" ah, without going into the details . . . don't, don't lie to them to the extent to say there is no involvement, but just say this is sort of a comedy of errors, bizarre, without getting into it, "the President believes that it is going to open the whole Bay of Pigs thing up again. And, ah because these people are plugging for, for keeps and that they should call the FBI in and say that we wish for the country, don't go any further into this case," period!

Haldeman: OK.

Nixon: That's the way to put it, do it straight [Unintelligible].

Haldeman: Get more done for our cause by the opposition than by us at this point.

Nixon: You think so?

Haldeman: I think so, yeah.

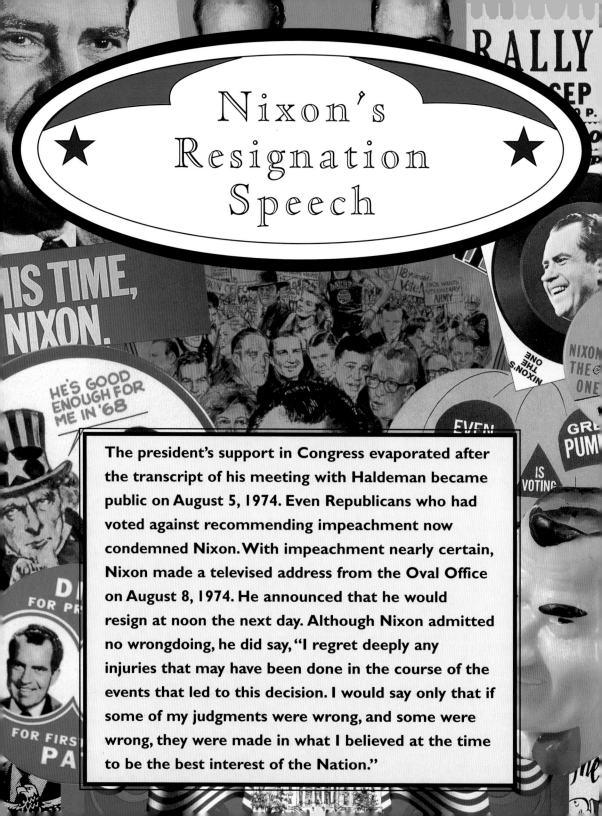

Nixon's Resignation Speech

The president's support in Congress evaporated after the transcript of his meeting with Haldeman became public on August 5, 1974. Even Republicans who had voted against recommending impeachment now condemned Nixon. With impeachment nearly certain, Nixon made a televised address from the Oval Office on August 8, 1974. He announced that he would resign at noon the next day. Although Nixon admitted no wrongdoing, he did say, "I regret deeply any injuries that may have been done in the course of the events that led to this decision. I would say only that if some of my judgments were wrong, and some were wrong, they were made in what I believed at the time to be the best interest of the Nation."

Good evening.

This is the 37th time I have spoken to you from this office, where so many decisions have been made that shaped the history of this Nation. Each time I have done so to discuss with you some matter that I believe affected the national interest.

In all the decisions I have made in my public life, I have always tried to do what was best for the Nation. Throughout the long and difficult period of Watergate, I have felt it was my duty to persevere, to make every possible effort to complete the term of office to which you elected me.

In the past few days, however, it has become evident to me that I no longer have a strong enough political base in the Congress to justify continuing that effort. As long as there was such a base, I felt strongly that it was necessary to see the constitutional process through to its conclusion, that to do otherwise would be unfaithful to the spirit of that deliberately difficult process and a dangerously destabilizing precedent for the future.

But with the disappearance of that base, I now believe that the constitutional purpose has been served, and there is no longer a need for the process to be prolonged.

I would have preferred to carry through to the finish whatever the personal agony it would have involved, and my family unanimously urged me to do so. But the interest of the Nation must always come before any personal considerations.

From the discussions I have had with Congressional and other leaders, I have concluded that because of the Watergate matter I might not have the support of the Congress that I would consider necessary to back the very difficult decisions and carry out the duties of this office in the way the interests of the Nation would require.

I have never been a quitter. To leave office before my term is completed is abhorrent to every instinct in my body. But as President, I must put the interest of America first. America needs a full-time President and a full-time Congress, particularly at this time with problems we face at home and abroad.

To continue to fight through the months ahead for my personal vindication would almost totally absorb the time and attention of both the President and the Congress in a period when our entire focus should be on the great issues of peace abroad and prosperity without inflation at home.

Therefore, I shall resign the Presidency effective at noon tomorrow. Vice President Ford will be sworn in as President at that hour in this office.

As I recall the high hopes for America with which we began this second term, I feel a great sadness that I will not be here in this office working on your behalf to achieve those hopes in the next two-and-a-half years. But in turning over direction of the Government to Vice President Ford, I know, as I told the Nation when I nominated him for that office ten months ago, that the leadership of America will be in good hands.

In passing this office to the Vice President, I also do so with the profound sense of the weight of responsibility that will fall on his shoulders tomorrow and, therefore, of the understanding, the patience, the cooperation he will need from all Americans.

As he assumes that responsibility, he will deserve the help and the support of all of us. As we look to the future, the first essential is to begin healing the wounds of this Nation, to put the bitterness and divisions of the recent past behind us, and to rediscover those shared ideals that lie at the heart of our strength and unity as a great and as a free people.

By taking this action, I hope that I will have hastened the start of that process of healing which is so desperately needed in America.

I regret deeply any injuries that may have been done in the course of the events that led to this decision. I would say only that if some of my judgments were wrong, and some were wrong, they were made in what I believed at the time to be the best interest of the Nation.

To those who have stood with me during these past difficult months, to my family, my friends, to many others who joined in supporting my cause because they believed it was right, I will be eternally grateful for your support.

And to those who have not felt able to give me your support, let me say I leave with no bitterness toward those who have opposed me, because all of us, in the final analysis, have been concerned with the good of the country, however our judgments might differ.

So, let us all now join together in affirming that common commitment and in helping our new President succeed for the benefit of all Americans.

I shall leave this office with regret at not completing my term, but with gratitude for the privilege of serving as your President for the past five-and-a-half years. These years have been a momentous time in the history of our Nation and the world. They have been a time of achievement in which we can all be proud, achievements that represent the shared efforts of the Administration, the Congress, and the people.

But the challenges ahead are equally great, and they, too, will require the support and the efforts of the Congress and the people working in cooperation with the new Administration.

We have ended America's longest war, but in the work of securing a lasting peace in the world, the goals ahead are even more far-reaching and more difficult. We must complete a structure of peace so that it will be said of this generation, our generation of Americans, by the people of all nations, not only that we ended one war but that we prevented future wars.

We have unlocked the doors that for a quarter of a century stood between the United States and the People's Republic of China.

We must now ensure that the one quarter of the world's people who live in the People's Republic of China will be and remain not our enemies but our friends.

In the Middle East, 100 million people in the Arab countries, many of whom have considered us their enemy for nearly 20 years, now look on us as their friends. We must continue to build on that friendship so that peace can settle at last over the Middle East and so that the cradle of civilization will not become its grave.

Together with the Soviet Union we have made the crucial breakthroughs that have begun the process of limiting nuclear arms. But we must set as our goal not just limiting but reducing and finally destroying these terrible weapons so that they cannot destroy civilization and so that the threat of nuclear war will no longer hang over the world and the people.

We have opened the new relation with the Soviet Union. We must continue to develop and expand that new relationship so that the two strongest nations of the world will live together in cooperation rather than confrontation.

Around the world, in Asia, in Africa, in Latin America, in the Middle East, there are millions of people who live in terrible poverty, even starvation. We must keep as our goal turning away from production for war and expanding production for peace so that people everywhere on this earth can at last look forward in their children's time, if not in our own time, to having the necessities for a decent life.

Here in America, we are fortunate that most of our people have not only the blessings of liberty but also the means to live full and good and, by the world's standards, even abundant lives. We must press on, however, toward a goal of not only more and better jobs but of full opportunity for every American and of what we are striving so hard right now to achieve, prosperity without inflation.

For more than a quarter of a century in public life I have shared in the turbulent history of this era. I have fought for what I believed in. I have tried to the best of my ability to discharge those duties and meet those responsibilities that were entrusted to me.

Sometimes I have succeeded and sometimes I have failed, but always I have taken heart from what Theodore Roosevelt once said about the man in the arena, "whose face is marred by dust and sweat and blood, who strives valiantly, who errs and comes short again and again because there is not effort without error and shortcoming, but who does actually strive to do the deed, who knows the great enthusiasms, the great devotions, who spends himself in a worthy cause, who at the best knows in the end the triumphs of high achievements and who at the worst, if he fails, at least fails while daring greatly."

I pledge to you tonight that as long as I have a breath of life in my body, I shall continue in that spirit. I shall continue to work for the great causes to which I have been dedicated throughout my years as a Congressman, a Senator, a Vice President, and President, the cause of peace not just for America but among all nations, prosperity, justice, and opportunity for all of our people.

There is one cause above all to which I have been devoted and to which I shall always be devoted for as long as I live.

When I first took the oath of office as President five-and-a-half years ago, I made this sacred commitment, to "consecrate my office, my energies, and all the wisdom I can summon to the cause of peace among nations."

I have done my very best in all the days since to be true to that pledge. As a result of these efforts, I am confident that the world is a safer place today, not only for the people of America but for the people of all nations, and that all of our children have a better chance than before of living in peace rather than dying in war.

This, more than anything, is what I hoped to achieve when I sought the Presidency. This, more than anything, is what I hope will be my legacy to you, to our country, as I leave the Presidency.

To have served in this office is to have felt a very personal sense of kinship with each and every American. In leaving it, I do so with this prayer: May God's grace be with you in all the days ahead.

★ Ford's Remarks on ★ Becoming President

"Our long national nightmare is over," proclaimed Gerald R. Ford on August 9, 1974, after taking the oath of office as the 38th president of the United States. The new president was personable, hardworking, and honest. To most Americans, these were attractive qualities after their recent political experience. On no issue—domestic or foreign—were there any discernible differences between Ford and Nixon. Since 1949, when Ford was elected to the House of Representatives, he had reflected the views of his conservative Michigan constituency. As House minority leader, he had won the respect of Democrats and Republicans because of his candor and even temper. Ford is the first person in American history to be appointed to fill a vacancy in the vice presidency and the only vice president to become president upon the resignation of the president—and the first president to reach the White House through the procedure established by the Twenty-fifth Amendment (1967).

The oath that I have taken is the same oath that was taken by George Washington and by every President under the Constitution. But I assume the Presidency under extraordinary circumstances never before experienced by Americans. This is an hour of history that troubles our minds and hurts our hearts.

Therefore, I feel it is my first duty to make an unprecedented compact with my countrymen. Not an inaugural address, not a fireside chat, not a campaign speech—just a little straight talk among friends. And I intend it to be the first of many.

I am acutely aware that you have not elected me as your President by your ballots, and so I ask you to confirm me as your President with your prayers. And I hope that such prayers will also be the first of many.

If you have not chosen me by secret ballot, neither have I gained office by any secret promises. I have not campaigned either for the Presidency or the Vice Presidency. I have not subscribed to any partisan platform. I am indebted to no man, and only to one woman—my dear wife—as I begin this very difficult job.

I have not sought this enormous responsibility, but I will not shirk it. Those who nominated and confirmed me as Vice President were my friends and are my friends. They were of both parties, elected by all the people and acting under the Constitution in their name. It is only fitting then that I should pledge to them and to you that I will be the President of all the people.

Thomas Jefferson said the people are the only sure reliance for the preservation of our liberty. And down the years, Abraham Lincoln renewed this American article of faith asking, "Is there any better way or equal hope in the world?"

I intend, on Monday next, to request of the Speaker of the House of Representatives and the President pro tempore of the Senate the privilege of appearing before the Congress to share with my former colleagues and with you, the American people, my views on the priority business of the Nation and to solicit your views and their views. And may I say to the Speaker and the others, if I could meet with you right after these remarks, I would appreciate it.

Even though this is late in an election year, there is no way we can go forward except together and no way anybody can win except by serving the people's urgent needs. We cannot stand still or slip backwards. We must go forward now together.

To the peoples and the governments of all friendly nations, and I hope that could encompass the whole world, I pledge an uninterrupted and sincere search for peace. America will remain strong and united, but its strength will remain dedicated to the safety and sanity of the entire family of man, as well as to our own precious freedom.

I believe that truth is the glue that holds government together, not only our Government but civilization itself. That bond, though strained, is unbroken at home and abroad.

In all my public and private acts as your President, I expect to follow my instincts of openness and candor with full confidence that honesty is always the best policy in the end.

My fellow Americans, our long national nightmare is over.

Our Constitution works; our great Republic is a government of laws and not of men. Here the people rule. But there is a higher Power, by whatever name we honor Him, who ordains not only righteousness but love, not only justice but mercy.

As we bind up the internal wounds of Watergate, more painful and more poisonous than those of foreign wars, let us restore the golden rule to our political process, and let brotherly love purge our hearts of suspicion and of hate.

In the beginning, I asked you to pray for me. Before closing, I ask again your prayers, for Richard Nixon and for his family. May our former President,

Less than two years after he won reelection by as huge a margin as any in American history, Nixon resigned from office in defeat and humiliation.

A Day in History—10 Pages

Special Index on Page 5

WEATHER
Tonight: Clear, 60s.
Tomorrow:
Sunny, 70s.
Fair Sunday.
Air: Unhealthful

New York Post

FOUNDED 1801, THE OLDEST CONTINUOUSLY PUBLISHED DAILY IN THE UNITED STATES.

Vol. 173
No. 224

NEW YORK, FRIDAY, AUGUST 9, 1974
© 1974 New York Post Corporation

20 Cents

WALL ST.
CLOSING

FINAL

LATE
SPORTS

FORD: *Takes Oath As President*

He takes the reins of power.

NIXON: *His Troubles Aren't Over*

During his tearful farewell today.

who brought peace to millions, find it for himself. May God bless and comfort his wonderful wife and daughters, whose love and loyalty will forever be a shining legacy to all who bear the lonely burdens of the White House.

I can only guess at those burdens, although I have witnessed at close hand the tragedies that befell three Presidents and the lesser trials of others.

With all the strength and all the good sense I have gained from life, with all the confidence my family, my friends, and my dedicated staff impart to me, and with the good will of countless Americans I have encountered in recent visits to 40 States, I now solemnly reaffirm my promise I made to you last December 6—to uphold the Constitution, to do what is right as God gives me to see the right, and to do the very best I can for America.

God helping me, I will not let you down.

Thank you.

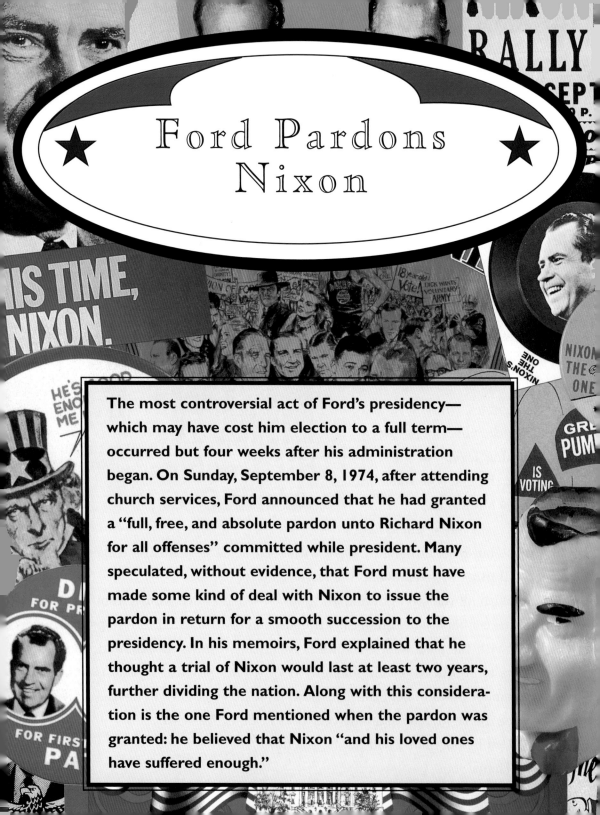

Ford Pardons Nixon

The most controversial act of Ford's presidency—which may have cost him election to a full term—occurred but four weeks after his administration began. On Sunday, September 8, 1974, after attending church services, Ford announced that he had granted a "full, free, and absolute pardon unto Richard Nixon for all offenses" committed while president. Many speculated, without evidence, that Ford must have made some kind of deal with Nixon to issue the pardon in return for a smooth succession to the presidency. In his memoirs, Ford explained that he thought a trial of Nixon would last at least two years, further dividing the nation. Along with this consideration is the one Ford mentioned when the pardon was granted: he believed that Nixon "and his loved ones have suffered enough."

By the President of the United States of America, a Proclamation:

Richard Nixon became the thirty-seventh President of the United States on January 20, 1969, and was reelected in 1972 for a second term by the electors of forty-nine of the fifty states. His term in office continued until his resignation on August 9, 1974.

Pursuant to resolutions of the House of Representatives, its Committee on the Judiciary conducted an inquiry and investigation on the impeachment of the President extending over more than eight months. The hearings of the Committee and its deliberations, which received wide national publicity over television, radio, and in printed media, resulted in votes adverse to Richard Nixon on recommended Articles of Impeachment.

As a result of certain acts or omissions occurring before his resignation from the Office of President, Richard Nixon has become liable to possible indictment and trial for offenses against the United States. Whether or not he shall be so prosecuted depends on findings of the appropriate grand jury and on the discretion of the authorized prosecutor. Should an indictment ensue, the accused shall then be entitled to a fair trial by an impartial jury, as guaranteed to every individual by the Constitution.

It is believed that a trial of Richard Nixon, if it became necessary, could not fairly begin until a year or more has elapsed. In the meantime, the tranquility to which this nation has been restored by the events of recent weeks could be irreparably lost by the prospects of bringing to trial a former President of the United States. The prospects of such trial will cause prolonged and divisive debate over the propriety of exposing to further punishment and degradation a man who has already paid the unprecedented penalty of relinquishing the highest elective office of the United States.

Now, Therefore, I, Gerald R. Ford, President of the United States, pursuant to the pardon power conferred upon me by Article II, Section 2, of the Constitution, have granted and by these presents do grant a full, free, and absolute pardon unto Richard Nixon for all offenses against the United States which he, Richard Nixon, has committed or may have committed or taken part in during the period from January 20, 1969, through August 9, 1974.

In Witness Whereof, I have hereunto set my hand this eighth day of September, in the year of our Lord nineteen hundred and seventy-four, and of the Independence of the United States of America the one hundred and ninety-ninth.

After the exhausting Watergate ordeal, the good feelings of the first weeks of President Ford's administration came as a relief. Ford's selection of Governor Nelson Rockefeller of New York as vice president pleased Republican moderates.

Nixon retired with his wife to their secluded estate at San Clemente, California. He wrote *RN: The Memoirs of Richard Nixon* (1978) and several books on international affairs. By the mid-1980s, Nixon seemed to have evolved into a nostalgic political figure, and by the 1990s, Watergate had become less of a benchmark for judging his presidency. He died in 1994. In retrospect, Nixon remains among the most controversial political figures since World War II and among the most important presidents of the twentieth century.

Further Reading

GENERAL REFERENCE

Israel, Fred L. *Student's Atlas of American Presidential Elections, 1789–1996*. Washington, D.C.: Congressional Quarterly Books, 1998.

Levy, Peter B., editor. *100 Key Documents in American History*. Westport, Conn.: Praeger, 1999.

Mieczkowski, Yarek. *The Routledge Historical Atlas of Presidential Elections*. New York: Routledge, 2001.

Polsby, Nelson W., and Aaron Wildavsky. *Presidential Elections: Strategies and Structures of American Politics*. 10th edition. New York: Chatham House, 2000.

Watts, J. F., and Fred L. Israel, editors. *Presidential Documents*. New York: Routledge, 2000.

Widmer, Ted. *The New York Times Campaigns: A Century of Presidential Races*. New York: DK Publishing, 2000.

POLITICAL AMERICANA REFERENCE

Cunningham, Noble E. Jr. *Popular Images of the Presidency: From Washington to Lincoln*. Columbia: University of Missouri Press, 1991.

Melder, Keith. *Hail to the Candidate: Presidential Campaigns from Banners to Broadcasts*. Washington, D.C.: Smithsonian Institution Press, 1992.

Schlesinger, Arthur M. jr., Fred L. Israel, and David J. Frent. *Running for President: The Candidates and their Images*. 2 vols. New York: Simon and Schuster, 1994.

Warda, Mark. *100 Years of Political Campaign Collectibles*. Clearwater, Fla.: Galt Press, 1996.

THE ELECTION OF 1968
and the Administration of Richard M. Nixon

Chester, Lewis. *An American Melodrama: The Presidential Campaign of 1968*. New York: Viking, 1969.

Cook, Rhodes. *United States Presidential Primary Elections 1968–1996: A Handbook of Election Statistics*. Washington, D.C.: Congressional Quarterly, 2000.

Dover, E. D. *Presidential Elections in the Television Age, 1960–1992*. Westport, Conn.: Praeger Publishing, 1994.

Goodwin, Doris Kearns. *Lyndon Johnson and the American Dream*. New York: St. Martin's Press, 1991.

Gould, Lewis L. *1968: The Election that Changed America*. Chicago: Ivan R. Dee, 1993.

Hoeh, David Charles. *1968—McCarthy—New Hampshire: "I Hear America Singing."* Red Wing, Minn.: Lone Oak Press, 1994.

Humphrey, Hubert N. *The Education of a Public Man: My Life and Politics*. Minneapolis: University of Minnesota Press, 1992.

McGillivray, Alice V., Richard M. Scammon, and Rhodes Cook. *America at the Polls 1960–1996: Kennedy to Clinton: A Handbook of American Presidential Election Statistics*. Washington, D.C.: Congressional Quarterly, 1998.

McGinnis, Joe. *The Selling of the President 1968*. New York: Trident Press, 1969.

Nixon, Richard M. *RN: The Memoirs of Richard Nixon*. Carmichael, Calif.: Touchstone Books, 1990.

Reeves, Richard. *President Nixon: Alone in the White House*. New York: Simon and Schuster, 2001.

White, Theodore H. *The Making of the President 1968*. New York: Atheneum, 1969.

Witcover, Jules. *85 Days: The Last Campaign of Robert Kennedy*. New York: Putnam, 1969.

INDEX

Numbers in **bold italics** refer to captions.

The EDITORS

ARTHUR M. SCHLESINGER JR. holds the Albert Schweitzer Chair in the Humanities at the Graduate Center of the City University of New York. He is the author of more than a dozen books, including *The Age of Jackson*; *The Vital Center; The Age of Roosevelt* (3 vols.); *A Thousand Days: John F. Kennedy in the White House; Robert Kennedy and His Times; The Cycles of American History;* and *The Imperial Presidency.* Professor Schlesinger served as Special Assistant to President Kennedy (1961–63). His numerous awards include: the Pulitzer Prize for History; the Pulitzer Prize for Biography; two National Book Awards; The Bancroft Prize; and the American Academy of Arts and Letters Gold Medal for History.

FRED L. ISRAEL is professor emeritus of American history, City College of New York. He is the author of *Nevada's Key Pittman* and has edited *The War Diary of Breckinridge Long* and *Major Peace Treaties of Modern History, 1648–1975* (5 vols.) He holds the Scribe's Award from the American Bar Association for his joint editorship of the *Justices of the United States Supreme Court* (4 vols.). For more than 25 years Professor Israel has compiled and edited the Gallup Poll into annual reference volumes.

DAVID J. FRENT is the president of Political Americana Auctions, Oakhurst, NJ. With his wife, Janice, he has assembled the nation's foremost private collection of political campaign memorabilia. Mr. Frent has designed exhibits for corporations, the Smithsonian Institution, and the United States Information Agency. A member of the board of directors of the American Political Items Collectors since 1972, he was elected to its Hall of Fame for his "outstanding contribution to preserving and studying our political heritage."